United States Government Accountability Office

Report to Congressional Requesters

I0448371

August 2013

OIL AND GAS DEVELOPMENT

BLM Needs Better Data to Track Permit Processing Times and Prioritize Inspections

GAO Highlights

Highlights of GAO-13-572, a report to congressional requesters

OIL AND GAS DEVELOPMENT

BLM Needs Better Data to Track Permit Processing Times and Prioritize Inspections

Why GAO Did This Study

BLM has key responsibilities for the development of federal oil and gas resources, including processing APDs. In 2005, GAO reported that the total number of APDs approved by BLM had increased, and as a result, BLM staff had less time for activities such as environmental inspections.

GAO was asked to review BLM's processing of APDs and efforts to protect the environment since then. This report examines, from fiscal years 2007 to 2012, (1) changes in BLM's permitting workload; (2) actions BLM has taken to manage its oil and gas permitting workload and challenges, if any, that remain; and (3) actions BLM has taken to mitigate the environmental impact of developing federal oil and gas resources, and challenges, if any, that remain. GAO analyzed BLM data on APDs and environmental inspections, from fiscal years 2007 to 2012, and interviewed officials at 11 BLM field offices selected to reflect a range of characteristics, including geographic representation.

What GAO Recommends

GAO recommends, among other things, that BLM should report to Congress on the results of a pilot project to improve APD processing and recommend whether it should be implemented throughout the United States; improve the completeness and accuracy of data on processing of APDs; and take steps to improve its ability to identify wells that are a high priority for environmental inspection. In commenting on a draft of this report, the Department of the Interior generally agreed with GAO's recommendations.

View GAO-13-572. For more information, contact Frank Rusco at (202) 512-3841 or ruscof@gao.gov.

What GAO Found

Bureau of Land Management (BLM) data indicate that BLM received about half as many applications for permit to drill (APD) for federal oil and gas resources in fiscal year 2012 as it had in fiscal year 2007. The decline in APDs since 2007 was driven by declines in natural gas and coalbed methane APDs on federal lands even while oil development on federal lands increased significantly. The reasons BLM officials and industry representatives cited for these changes in APDs include, among other things, a general industry move toward developing gas in shale formations using horizontal drilling and hydraulic fracturing; shale development has largely occurred on state and private lands, where shale resources are predominately located. However, the number of APDs has varied by BLM location, with 23 of 33 BLM offices seeing declines, 9 offices seeing increases, and 1 office seeing no change in APDs.

BLM has taken actions to improve management of its oil and gas permitting workload, including revising its permitting rule in 2007 and implementing a pilot project to improve APD processing that increased funding and staff in seven BLM offices. It is unclear whether the pilot project has met its goals as BLM has neither completed an assessment of the project in the past 5 years, nor reported to Congress, as required by the Energy Policy Act of 2005, on the results of the project along with a recommendation about implementing the project throughout the United States. Further, in a 2013 internal memorandum, BLM reported that it has been unable to consistently process completed APDs within the 30-day deadline required by the act. GAO found that BLM's central oil and gas database was missing certain data needed to assess compliance with this deadline and contained other inaccurate APD processing data. Without complete data on approved APDs, GAO could not perform a comprehensive assessment of the amount of time it took BLM to process APDs from their date of receipt to date of approval. Without accurate data on the amount of time it takes to process APDs, BLM does not have the information it needs to make adjustments that could improve its operations.

To mitigate the environmental impact of oil and gas development, BLM increased the number of environmental inspections it conducted of federal oil and gas wells and facilities from 10,941 in fiscal year 2007 to 17,866 in fiscal year 2012. BLM attributed the increase to revised guidance, performance targets for staff, additional staff in some offices, and technological changes in the oil and gas industry that result in more wells on a single well pad, allowing for multiple inspections at one site. Nevertheless, BLM's environmental inspection prioritization process may not identify oil and gas wells that pose the greatest environmental risk because the agency's central oil and gas database does not include data on the environmental inspection history of many wells, and environmental inspection history is not one of the criteria that BLM staff use in prioritizing inspections. GAO's review of data on approximately 60,330 federal oil and gas wells found no record in BLM's database of 24,840 wells ever having received an environmental inspection. In addition, GAO found inconsistent documentation of inspections and enforcement actions across BLM offices.

_____ United States Government Accountability Office

Contents

Abbreviations

AFMSS	Automated Fluid Minerals Support System
APD	application for permit to drill
BLM	Bureau of Land Management
COA	conditions of approval
FLPMA	Federal Land Policy and Management Act of 1976
FOGRMA	Federal Oil and Gas Royalty Management Act of 1982
INC	Incident of Noncompliance
IT	information technology
NEPA	National Environmental Policy Act of 1969

August 23, 2013

The Honorable Peter DeFazio
Ranking Member
Committee on Natural Resources
House of Representatives

The Honorable Edward J. Markey
United States Senate

Over the past decade, the development of the nation's domestic sources of oil and natural gas—including on state, private, and federal lands—has intensified. At the same time, several changes have occurred in the oil and gas sector, such as shifts in oil and natural gas prices and technological advancements in horizontal drilling techniques combined with hydraulic fracturing.[1] For example, horizontal drilling combined with hydraulic fracturing has resulted in the substantial growth of domestic onshore shale oil and shale gas production from 2007 to 2011.[2] The changing dynamics of the onshore oil and gas sector contribute to challenges faced by the Department of the Interior's Bureau of Land Management (BLM), which manages onshore federal oil and gas resources. Specifically the Federal Land Policy and Management Act of 1976 (FLPMA), as amended, directs Interior to manage federal land for multiple uses, such as recreation and mineral extraction, while also taking any action required to prevent the "unnecessary or undue degradation" of federal land, including federal land that has been leased for oil and gas operations. The challenges BLM faces in managing the development of federal oil and gas resources while also mitigating the environmental impacts of this development have generated concern among some federal and state government officials, conservationists, and oil and gas companies about the balance between oil and gas development and the use of these federal lands for other purposes.

---

[1]Hydraulic fracturing is a process in which water, sand, and chemical additives are injected under high pressure to create and maintain fractures in underground formations in order to extract oil and gas resources. When combined with horizontal drilling, hydraulic fracturing allows operators to fracture the rock formation along the entire horizontal portion of a well, increasing the number of pathways through which oil or gas can flow.

[2]See GAO, *Oil and Gas: Information on Shale Resources, Development, and Environmental and Public Health Risks*, GAO-12-732 (Washington, D.C.: Sept. 5, 2012).

Under the Mineral Leasing Act of 1920, as amended, and other statutes, BLM issues leases for the development of oil and gas resources where authorized on and under BLM-managed federal land, under other federal agencies' lands, and under private land for which the federal government holds mineral rights—amounting to roughly 700 million subsurface acres. Companies or individuals (referred to in this report as operators) holding leases for oil and gas development must submit an application for permit to drill (APD) to BLM and obtain approval before preparing land or drilling new oil or gas wells. After receiving an APD, BLM generally communicates with operators until they provide all of the required documents. The Energy Policy Act of 2005,[3] among other things, requires BLM to approve or defer the APD within 30 days after the operator has submitted a complete APD. BLM's process for reviewing an APD includes several key steps. For example, BLM generally reviews the APD to mitigate or avoid adverse impacts on the land, air, water, vegetation, and wildlife. Additionally, under its regulations, BLM is to ensure that the operator's plans comply with relevant laws and regulations under BLM's jurisdiction.[4] In addition, BLM is to review lease requirements, known as stipulations. BLM staff also are to review the APD to determine if any conditions of approval (COA)—such as protections for wildlife habitat, management of invasive species, or testing of well control equipment—should be included in the APD. Once BLM approves the APD, and operators have obtained any necessary state permits or approvals, operators may drill, subject to the conditions of the APD.

BLM is responsible for requiring that operators comply with the terms of APDs, including COAs, during the entire life cycle of every well, and can take enforcement action if operators do not comply. Under the Federal Oil and Gas Royalty Management Act of 1982 (FOGRMA), as amended,[5]

---

[3]Pub. L. No. 109-58, 119 Stat. 594 (2005).

[4]BLM officials said that they generally review APDs for compliance with laws that are relevant to BLM's jurisdiction, but not for laws that fall under the jurisdiction of other agencies, such as the Environmental Protection Agency, or for state laws and regulations. In some cases, BLM and states may regulate similar activities; in such cases, operators must comply with the more stringent regulation. For additional information on selected state requirements, see, GAO, *Unconventional Oil and Gas Development: Key Environmental and Public Health Requirements*, GAO-12-874 (Washington, D.C.: Sept. 5, 2012).

[5]Pub. L. No. 97–451, 96 Stat. 2447 (1993), codified as amended at 30 U.S.C. §§ 1701 et seq. (2013).

BLM has the authority to inspect federal oil and gas sites, including well pads and production facilities. According to the agency's handbook for its inspection and enforcement program, BLM must ensure that oil and gas operations on federal lands are prudently conducted in a manner that ensures protection of the surface and subsurface environment.[6] Among the inspections conducted by BLM are environmental inspections that, among other things, ensure that (1) sensitive species are not disturbed during the construction of a well pad, (2) pits designed to hold the waste by-products of drilling activities are appropriately constructed and maintained, (3) significant erosion is not occurring on the well site, and (4) disturbed lands are properly reclaimed to as close to original condition as practical. If BLM determines through an inspection that a violation of a restriction or requirement of the APD occurred or is occurring, the agency can, depending on the violation, issue assessments or civil penalties or take other enforcement action.

In 2005, we reported on aspects of BLM's responsibilities for onshore oil and gas development.[7] Specifically, we reported that an increase in oil and gas operations on federal lands had lessened BLM's ability to meet its responsibilities for mitigating the environmental impacts of oil and gas development. We found that from fiscal year 1999 to fiscal year 2004, the total number of APDs approved by BLM more than tripled—from 1,803 to 6,399—and BLM officials in five out of eight field offices that we visited said that staff had to devote more time to processing APDs, leaving less time for conducting environmental inspections.

You asked us to review BLM actions taken after our 2005 report with respect to processing APDs for oil and gas resources on federal lands and mitigating environmental impacts. The objectives of this review were to determine, from fiscal years 2007 to 2012, (1) what changes have occurred in BLM's oil and gas permitting workload; (2) what actions BLM has taken to manage its oil and gas permitting workload and what challenges, if any, remain; and (3) what actions BLM has taken to mitigate the surface environmental impact of developing federal oil and

---

[6]U.S. Department o the Interior, BLM, *2009 Inspection and Enforcement Documentation and Strategy Development Handbook* (Washington, D.C., 2009).

[7]GAO, *Increased Permitting Activity Has Lessened BLM's Ability to Meet Its Environmental Protection Responsibilities,* GAO-05-418 (Washington, D.C.: June 17, 2005).

gas resources and what challenges, if any, remain. We focused on actions BLM has taken to mitigate surface environmental impacts. We did not analyze other areas of BLM's environmental efforts including land use planning, lease decisions, and inspections of subsurface activity.

To conduct this work, we reviewed federal laws and regulations regarding BLM's management of onshore oil and gas resources owned by the federal government. In addition, we obtained data from BLM's Automated Fluid Minerals Support System (AFMSS)—the central database that BLM uses to track oil and gas information on public land—including data on APDs received or approved and environmental inspections performed since fiscal year 2005. Since BLM's information technology (IT) systems for tracking data on oil and gas development on Indian Trust lands were shut down for various periods from 2001 to 2008 because of a lawsuit, we did not review data on APDs or environmental inspections for nonfederal wells located on Indian Trust lands. Consequently, the data on APDs presented in this report refer exclusively to APDs for federal oil and gas resources, and the data presented on environmental inspections refer exclusively to inspections that were performed on federal wells and facilities. To determine how BLM's permitting workload has changed, we analyzed the data on APDs received by BLM. We also analyzed BLM's data on approved APDs to assess the time it takes to process APDs from the date of receipt to the date of approval. To assess the reliability of the APD data, we performed electronic testing of the data and interviewed agency officials about the data. We determined that the APD data were sufficiently reliable to present results on the number of APDs received by BLM from fiscal years 2007 to 2012 and the average number of days it took BLM to process APDs from the date of receipt to the date of approval in fiscal year 2012. We determined that BLM's data on approved APDs were not sufficiently reliable to assess BLM's compliance with the required 30-day deadline to approve or defer completed APDs or to assess the number of days it took BLM to process APDs prior to fiscal year 2012. To evaluate BLM's efforts to mitigate the surface environmental impacts of oil and gas development, we analyzed BLM's data on environmental inspections performed on federal oil and gas wells and facilities. To assess the reliability of the environmental inspection data, we performed electronic testing and interviewed agency officials about the data. We determined that the environmental inspection data for fiscal years 2005 and 2006 were not sufficiently reliable for our purposes; as a result, we limited the scope of the environmental inspections analysis to fiscal years 2007 through 2012. We believe the AFMSS data for those years are sufficiently reliable for the purposes presented in this report. To be consistent with our presentation of the environmental inspection data, we also limited the scope of the APD data presented in this report to fiscal years 2007 to 2012. To identify actions BLM has taken to manage its permitting workload and to mitigate the environmental impact of oil and gas development on federal lands, we reviewed BLM guidance and documentation and interviewed officials in BLM's Washington, D.C., headquarters office. We selected a nonprobability sample of 11 BLM field offices that manage oil and gas development to contact and collect information about how each office manages its oil and gas program, including how the office reviews APDs for environmental mitigation purposes and inspects oil and gas activity on federal lands.[8] We selected the 11 offices to reflect different geographical locations and types of oil and gas resources managed. In fiscal year 2012, these offices accounted for about 68 percent of all APDs received by BLM for federal oil and gas resources and for about 52 percent of all environmental inspections performed by BLM. In addition, we interviewed officials from four BLM state offices, selected on the basis of their jurisdiction over some of the field offices we contacted. We also interviewed representatives from environmental organizations and energy industry organizations to obtain their perspectives on BLM's management of federal oil and gas resources. Appendix I describes our scope and methodology in more detail.

We conducted this performance audit from May 2012 to August 2013 in accordance with generally accepted government auditing standards. Those standards require that we plan and perform the audit to obtain sufficient, appropriate evidence to provide a reasonable basis for our findings and conclusions based on our audit objectives. We believe that the evidence obtained provides a reasonable basis for our findings and conclusions based on our audit objectives.

---

[8]Because this was a nonprobability sample, observations from interviews with these offices, taken alone, do not support generalizations about other offices. However, such observations provide illustrative examples of the types of challenges BLM faces in managing its permitting workload and mitigating the environmental impact of oil and gas development. We visited and interviewed officials in eight BLM field offices (Colorado River Valley, Little Snake, and White River in Colorado; Moab, Price, and Vernal in Utah; and Pinedale and Rock Springs in Wyoming) and interviewed officials by telephone in three additional field offices (Carlsbad and Farmington in New Mexico, and the North Dakota Field Office). During our site visits to the Colorado River Valley, Vernal, and Pinedale Field Offices, we observed BLM officials conduct environmental inspections of oil or gas wells and related facilities.

Background

This section discusses BLM's organizational structure for managing oil and gas development, provides an overview of the process for developing federal oil and gas resources, and describes BLM's inspection and enforcement program.

BLM's Organizational Structure for Managing Oil and Gas Development

Implementation of BLM's oil and gas program, including processing APDs and performing environmental inspections, primarily occurs at the field office level and is led by 33 BLM offices located primarily in the Mountain West.[9] BLM's headquarters, state, and district offices oversee and provide guidance and support to the field offices that implement BLM's oil and gas program. As of December 2012, BLM offices were responsible for managing nearly 92,600 wells involved in developing federal onshore oil and gas resources. BLM offices in two states—New Mexico and Wyoming—accounted for about 67 percent of the total wells and BLM offices in three other states—California, Colorado, and Utah—accounted for about 24 percent. BLM's remaining offices collectively accounted for about 9 percent of the total (see fig. 1).[10] Overall, the number of wells managed by BLM has increased since fiscal year 2007, when BLM reported managing about 79,970 wells.

[9]These 33 offices consist of 30 field offices, 1 field station—located in Hobbs (NM), which works closely with the Carlsbad (NM) Field Office—and 2 state offices, the BLM Alaska State Office and the BLM Nevada State Office, which oversee the development of federal oil and gas resources throughout their respective states. Some BLM offices in other locations have small oil and gas programs that are administered with the assistance of the 33 lead offices.

[10]The number of wells presented here does not include federal wells that have been abandoned by operators or nonfederal wells that are located on Indian Trust lands.

Figure 1: BLM's Lead Offices for Oil and Gas Development and the Number of Wells They Manage

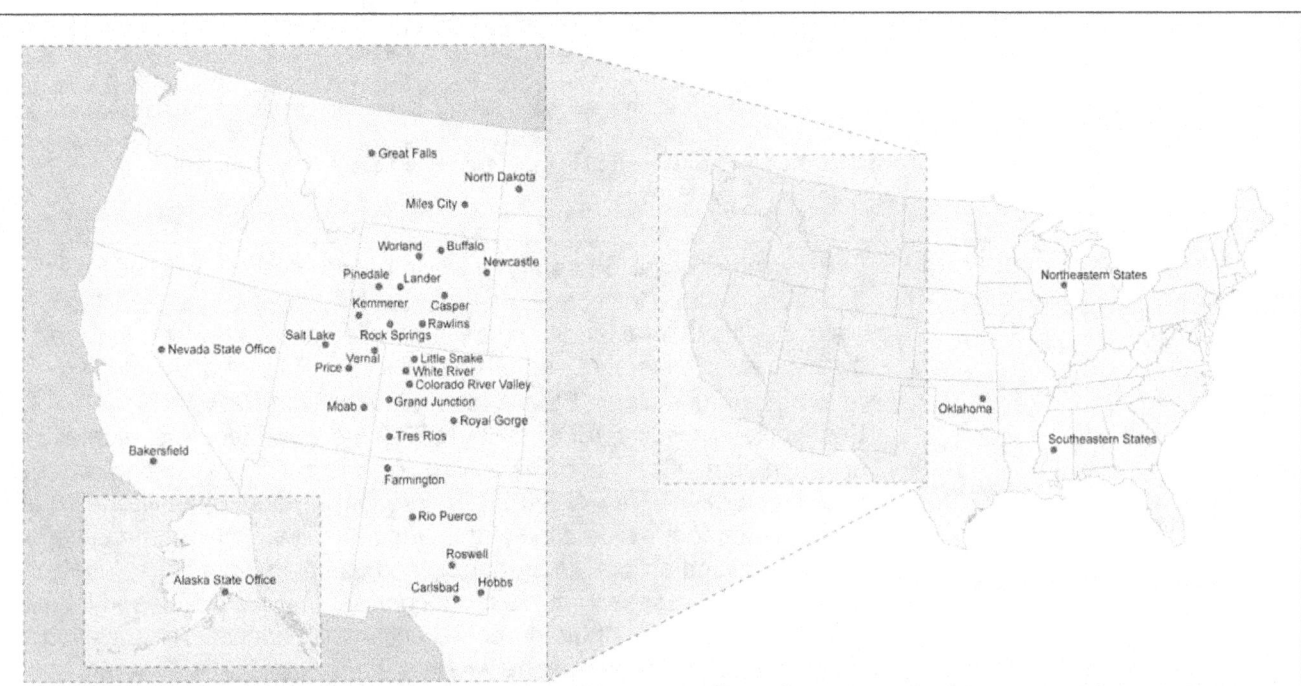

BLM office name (location)	Number of wells	BLM office name (location)	Number of wells
Farmington Field Office (NM)	14,732	North Dakota Field Office (ND)	1,404
Buffalo Field Office (WY)	12,607	Great Falls Oil and Gas Field Office (MT)	1,402
Carlsbad Field Office (NM)	8,425	Northeastern States Field Office (WI)	1,182
Bakersfield Field Office (CA)	7,930	Southeastern States Field Office (MS)	988
Vernal Field Office (UT)	6,643	Lander Field Office (WY)	908
Pinedale Field Office (WY)	5,527	Kemmerer Field Office (WY)	797
Hobbs Field Station (NM)[a]	4,802	Moab Field Office (UT)	680
Casper Field Office (WY)	3,546	Price Field Office (UT)	662
Worland Field Office (WY)	2,858	Rio Puerco Field Office (NM)	555
Rawlins Field Office (WY)	2,477	Little Snake Field Office (CO)	554
White River Field Office (CO)	2,369	Grand Junction Field Office (CO)	514
Colorado River Valley Field Office (CO)	2,358	Royal Gorge Field Office (CO)	454
Newcastle Field Office (WY)	1,597	Tres Rios Field Office (CO)	397
Roswell Field Office (NM)	1,519	Nevada State Office (NV)	119
Rock Springs Field Office (WY)	1,489	Alaska State Office (AK)	113
Miles City Field Office (MT)	1,481	Salt Lake Field Office (UT)	79
Oklahoma Field Office (OK)	1,417	**Total (all offices)**	**92,585[b]**

Sources: GAO analysis of BLM data; Map Resources (map).

Note: The data presented in this figure include (1) wells that were located on lands whose surface is managed by BLM and that were in a producible or service status (i.e., wells that were physically and mechanically capable of producing oil or gas or that were used to support oil and gas operations through activities such as water disposal) as of December 18, 2012, and (2) wells that were located on lands whose surface is managed by other federal, state, or private entities, but which have mineral rights that are controlled by the federal government and that were in a produc ble or service status as of November 30, 2012. This figure does not include data on federal wells that have been abandoned or nonfederal wells located on Indian Trust lands. Some BLM field offices in other locations also have small oil and gas programs that are administered with the assistance of the 33 lead offices, and their well numbers are included in the totals presented in this figure for their respective lead office.

aStaff from the Carlsbad Field Office provide support to the Hobbs Field Station on some oil and gas activities, including processing APDs and performing environmental inspections.

bBLM also manages 14 additional federal wells that are not included in the total presented in this figure due to their database records listing multiple field offices for the same well.

Overview of the Process for Developing Federal Oil and Gas Resources

FLPMA requires the Secretary of the Interior to develop land use plans that are evaluated for potential revision at least every 5 years. These plans identify federal lands and mineral resources that will be available for oil and gas development and other activities.[11] As part of developing or revising land use plans, BLM is required under the National Environmental Policy Act of 1969 (NEPA), as amended, to evaluate likely environmental effects of decisions in the plan, such as selecting areas for oil and gas development. Generally, Interior prepares an environmental impact statement—a detailed statement of the likely environmental effects of the proposed action—in preparing land use plans, but it may use an environmental assessment—a more concise analysis developed if the environmental effect of the proposed action is unknown in association with other actions to determine whether the action is likely to affect the environment significantly.[12] BLM officials said the agency uses the land use plans and environmental impact statements to (1) help develop "reasonably foreseeable development scenarios" to estimate outcomes, such as the number of wells and likely surface disturbance that may occur under the land use plan; (2) identify lands open and closed to leasing; (3) identify resource protection measures such as lease stipulations and environmental best management practices; and (4) to establish monitoring protocols. Consistent with a completed land use plan and its associated environmental impact statement, BLM can offer for lease those mineral rights identified in the plan and hence deemed available for leasing.

[11]Revisions to land use plans are necessary if monitoring and evaluation findings, new data, new or revised policy, or changes in circumstances indicate that decisions for an entire plan or a major portion of a plan no longer serves as a useful guide for resource management. BLM, *Land Use Planning Handbook H-1601-1*, p. 46 (Washington, D.C.: 2005).

[12]Pub. L. No. 91-190, 83 Stat. 852 (1970), codified as amended at 42 U.S.C. §§ 4321-4347 (2013); see § 4332(2)(C)(i).

Operators that have obtained a lease must submit an APD to BLM and obtain BLM's approval before drilling any new oil or gas wells. Beginning in fiscal year 2008, Congress authorized BLM to collect a $4,000 processing fee from operators for each new oil and gas APD. This processing fee was increased by Congress to $6,500 per APD in fiscal year 2010; any fees collected are used by BLM and offset the agency's general fund appropriation. A complete APD must include, among other things, a Surface Use Plan of Operations with the operator's plan for reclaiming disturbed lands during production (known as interim reclamation) and upon final abandonment of the well site (known as final reclamation). The reclamation plan covers both interim and final reclamation, and it outlines the steps the operator proposes to take to reclaim the well site. Those steps may include recontouring the topography to better match the surrounding landscape, redistributing topsoil, and revegetating the site with native plant species.

Once BLM determines the APD is complete, it decides whether to approve the APD. BLM may approve the APD as submitted or approve it subject to certain COAs. According to BLM officials, COAs are generally attached to ensure environmental protection, safety, or conservation of mineral resources, and may be based on environmental best management practices. These environmental best management practices emphasize, among other things, the importance of interim steps to reclaim land during oil and gas production and the benefits of reclamation activities for mitigating the environmental impacts of oil and gas development.[13] The COAs can be general in nature or site-specific. Typically, a field office develops COAs over a number of years of active management of oil and gas development. They can address such topics as interim and final reclamation, protection of wildlife habitat or archeological and paleontological sites, noise reduction, wildfire suppression, or management of invasive species. After BLM approves an APD, the operator generally has a 2-year window before the APD expires during which the operator can drill the well and begin production, subject to any lease stipulations or COAs.[14] However, upon a written request from the operator, BLM may extend the APD for up to 2 years.

---

[13]U.S. Department of the Interior, BLM, *Surface Operating Standards and Guidelines for Oil and Gas Exploration and Development* (Washington, D.C., 2007).

[14]Oil and gas development on federal lands also must comply with applicable state laws.

GAO-13-572 BLM Oil and Gas Development

When an operator determines, and BLM agrees, that a well has no further economic value, the operator must plug the well and complete final reclamation by following the original or an amended reclamation plan for the well. BLM is then responsible for inspecting the site to ensure reclamation actions have taken place and for monitoring the success of the reclamation, a process that typically occurs over several years. Once BLM determines that reclamation has been completed, it approves a Final Abandonment Notice.[15] As we reported in February 2011, all operators are required to complete reclamation, but they do not always do so.[16] In these circumstances, BLM may use the bond the operator posted for the well to help defray some of the cost of completing reclamation. If the bond is not sufficient to cover well plugging and surface reclamation and there are no responsible or liable parties, the well is considered "orphaned," and BLM uses federal dollars to fund reclamation.

As we reported in February 2011, BLM is also concerned with the status of idle wells.[17] Under the Energy Policy Act of 2005, an idle well is defined as a well that has been nonoperational for at least 7 years and has no anticipated beneficial use. These are previously operating wells that an operator has decided not to operate for a period of time. In some instances, this may be because the operator is waiting for oil and gas prices to rise. In our February 2011 report, we found that idle wells have the potential to create environmental, safety, and public health hazards if they fall into disrepair, and that they are at greater risk than other wells of becoming orphan wells.[18] Following our February 2011 report, BLM issued revised guidance on its reviews of idle wells in September 2012.[19]

---

[15]In circumstances where the surface land is managed by another federal agency, BLM generally is to obtain the approval of the surface management agency prior to approving the Final Abandonment Notice. Where the surface land is owned by a state or private entity, BLM generally may consider the surface owner's views respecting the abandonment plan.

[16]GAO, *Oil and Gas Bonds: BLM Needs a Comprehensive Strategy to Better Manage Potential Oil and Gas Well Liability*, GAO-11-292 (Washington, D.C.: Feb. 25, 2011).

[17]GAO-11-292.

[18]GAO-11-292.

[19]As BLM was just beginning to implement this revised guidance during the course of our review, we did not include BLM's environmental mitigation efforts related to idle wells in this report.

| BLM's Inspection and Enforcement Program | To help ensure operators' compliance with all stipulations in the lease and COAs in the APD, as well as certain laws and regulations, BLM has an inspection and enforcement program. BLM's authority for inspecting wells is derived from FOGRMA, which requires the Secretary of the Interior to develop guidelines that specify the coverage and frequency of inspections. BLM's AFMSS database tracks data on federal oil and gas wells, including data on environmental inspections. |

Environmental inspections are BLM's primary mechanism to ensure operators' compliance with lease stipulations, and COAs related to the surface environment, and to initiate enforcement actions if needed. For example, BLM may perform environmental inspections to help ensure that operators are adhering to COAs designed to mitigate the impact of oil and gas development on sensitive species and their habitat. BLM guidance does not require environmental inspection of all wells, or specify when a well should have an environmental inspection. Instead, BLM guidance instructs field offices to conduct environmental inspections annually on all wells rated high priority due to environmental concerns. BLM's inspection and enforcement handbook instructs offices to determine high-priority environmental inspections based on criteria including whether (1) operations on a well or facility are in or adjacent to an area of special environmental sensitivity, such as near threatened or endangered species habitat; (2) operations occur in an area where noncompliance with lease stipulations or COAs could have a significant adverse impact on the environment; (3) the operator has a history of noncompliance with environmental requirements; (4) 6 months have elapsed since a new well was completed or since a well has been abandoned, to ensure that earthwork for reclamation has been completed; and (5) an operator has submitted a Final Abandonment Notice. Based on these criteria, BLM's 33 lead oil and gas offices are to develop annual targets for the number of high-priority environmental inspections they plan to conduct for (1) wells expected to be drilled, (2) wells already producing oil or gas, and (3) wells expected to be plugged and abandoned.

Environmental inspections typically are performed by BLM staff—such as natural resource specialists, environmental protection specialists, or other resource program specialists—with specific training in environmental issues. For the purpose of this report, we will refer to all BLM staff who perform environmental inspections as environmental staff. As shown in figure 2, environmental inspections can occur during any stage in the life cycle of a well.

Figure 2: BLM's Common Environmental Inspection Activities at Different Stages in the Life Cycle of a Well

Stage 1: Construction and drilling

Environmental inspection activities[a]

During the construction of a well pad, BLM may perform environmental inspections to ensure that, among other things, operators do not disturb lands outside of the boundaries identified in the application for permit to drill (APD); that the construction does not disturb sensitive species; and that any topsoil removed from the site is stored in accordance with the plan described in the APD.

During the drilling of a new well, BLM may perform environmental inspections to review the surface disposal methods the operator is using for the by-products of drilling activities—such as drilling fluids or mud—and to verify that pits or tanks are free of visible leaks and have been adequately fenced or netted to protect wildlife and livestock.

Stage 2: Production

Environmental inspection activities[b]

Within 6 months of when a new well is completed, BLM guidance instructs operators to complete the earthwork for interim reclamation and instructs BLM to perform an environmental inspection to ensure that this has been done properly. During the production stage, environmental inspections are also performed to ensure compliance with all other interim reclamation requirements outlined in the Surface Use Plan of Operations, including applicable conditions of approval.

Also, BLM may perform environmental inspections on producing wells to ensure that, among other things, no fluids are leaking into the environment; that wildlife mitigation measures (such as screens or nets) have been installed; and that the well pad is free of trash or debris.

Stage 3: Abandonment

Environmental inspection activities[c]

BLM guidance instructs operators to complete the earthwork for final reclamation within 6 months of a well being plugged and instructs BLM to perform an environmental inspection to ensure that this has been done properly. Also, before approving the final abandonment of a well, BLM's guidance calls for BLM to perform an environmental inspection to ensure that all of the surface reclamation standards required in the Surface Use Plan of Operations have been satisfied.

Source: GAO analysis of BLM documents and data; GAO (left-hand and center photos); BLM (right-hand photo).

[a]BLM may also perform other types of inspections during this stage that are not specifically related to the surface environment, such as inspections to witness tests of the well's blowout prevention equipment or to examine the cementing or casing of the well.

[b]BLM may also perform other types of inspections of a well when it is producing oil or gas, such as inspections to verify that the well equipment is working properly and that the production meters are accurately measuring and accounting for the full volume of oil and gas being produced by the well.

[c]During this stage, BLM staff may also perform inspections to observe and examine the plugging of the well hole. BLM does not track these inspections as environmental inspections.

BLM's inspection and enforcement handbook defines a violation as a noncompliance with a specific requirement outlined in federal regulations, onshore orders, or COAs, among other things, and a problem as a concern or issue identified during an inspection that is not covered by a specific regulatory requirement. If BLM staff determine that a violation has occurred, they can issue a formal Incident of Noncompliance (INC) violation notice. Depending on the severity of a violation, INCs can result in the operator being fined. For example, if BLM discovers that an operator has begun construction of a well pad on federal or Indian surface without having approval to do so, BLM is authorized to assess the operator $500 for each day that the violation existed, up to a maximum of $5,000. If BLM staff determine that a problem occurred or is occurring, they can issue a verbal warning or a written order. The handbook also instructs BLM staff to document any enforcement actions in AFMSS.

BLM's Permitting Workload Has Changed in Number, Type, and Location of APDs

BLM's permitting workload has changed from fiscal year 2007 to fiscal year 2012 in terms of the (1) number and type of APDs received and (2) their location.

Natural Gas and Coalbed Methane APDs Have Decreased from Fiscal Year 2007 to Fiscal Year 2012 and APDs for Oil Wells Have Increased

Our analysis of BLM data found that BLM received about half as many APDs for federal oil and gas resources in fiscal year 2012 (4,303) as in fiscal year 2007 (8,573). Nonetheless, the number of APDs received in fiscal year 2012 represented about a 4 percent increase over fiscal year 2010, which was the year during our review that BLM received the fewest APDs (4,121). The general decline in APDs since 2007 was most evident in the number of APDs BLM received for new natural gas and coalbed methane wells, which dropped by approximately 52 percent and 99 percent, respectively, from fiscal year 2007 to fiscal year 2012. In contrast, the number of APDs received for oil wells increased by approximately 70 percent, with about 1,300 APDs received in fiscal year 2007 to about 2,200 APDs received in fiscal year 2012.[20] Figure 3 shows the total number of APDs for federal oil and gas resources received by BLM each fiscal year from 2007 through 2012 and breaks down the

[20]Oil, gas, and coalbed methane APDs, collectively, represent at least 96 percent of all APDs that BLM received each fiscal year from 2007 through 2012. In addition, BLM received a small number of APDs for monitoring wells, injection wells, and other types of wells that are used to support oil and gas operations. Together, these well types represented from about 2 to 4 percent of the total number of APDs BLM received each year.

numbers of APDs received for coalbed methane, natural gas, oil, and other types of wells.

Figure 3: Number of Applications for Permit to Drill Received by BLM by Source, Fiscal Years 2007-2012

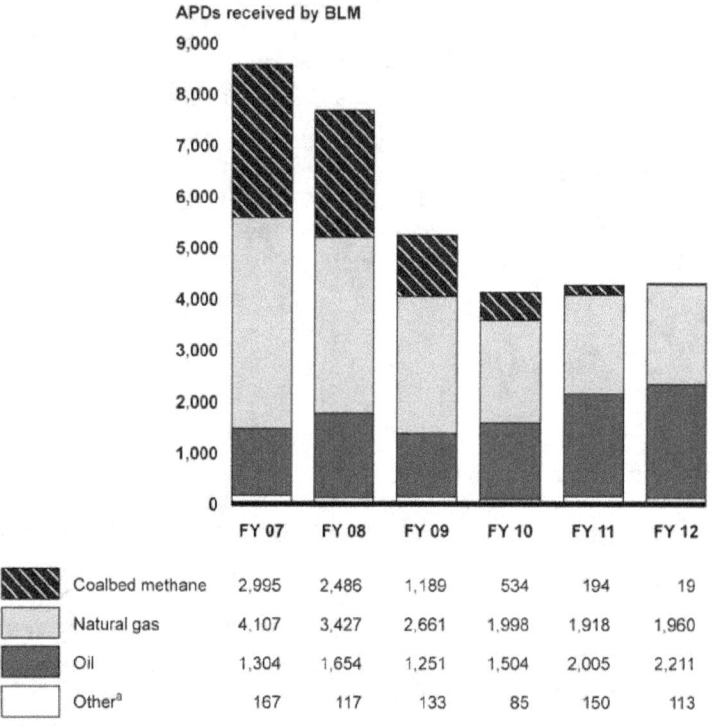

	FY 07	FY 08	FY 09	FY 10	FY 11	FY 12
Coalbed methane	2,995	2,486	1,189	534	194	19
Natural gas	4,107	3,427	2,661	1,998	1,918	1,960
Oil	1,304	1,654	1,251	1,504	2,005	2,211
Other[a]	167	117	133	85	150	113

Source: GAO analysis of BLM data.

Note: This figure presents data by fiscal year (FY) on applications for permit to drill (APD) for federal oil and gas resources and does not include APDs received by BLM for nonfederal oil and gas resources on Indian Trust lands. According to BLM officials, APDs for nonfederal oil and gas resources on Indian Trust lands are a sizeable portion of some BLM offices' permitting workload.

[a]Other includes, among other things, injection wells, which can be used to support oil and gas operations by injecting water or other fluids into oil- or gas-producing formations to increase the pressure in the formation and force additional oil or gas out of nearby producing wells.

BLM officials and oil and gas industry representatives we interviewed identified a variety of factors that can influence an operator's decision to develop oil and gas resources and that may provide context to the changes in BLM's permitting workload since fiscal year 2007. These factors include the following:

GAO-13-572 BLM Oil and Gas Development

- *The price of oil and natural gas.* Officials from the 11 BLM field offices we contacted said they consider the price of oil and natural gas to be a factor contributing to changes in their offices' permitting workload. For example, officials in 6 offices we contacted said that lower prices for natural gas have contributed to the decline in the number of natural gas and coalbed methane APDs their offices have received in recent years. In addition, officials from 5 offices located in areas where oil is being developed said that higher prices for oil have contributed to an increase in the number of oil APDs their offices have received. This is consistent with what we found in July 2010, when we reported on the relationship between fluctuations in oil and gas prices and development activities and found that changes in the prices of oil and gas closely paralleled changes in development activities from 1990 through 2009.[21] Specifically, we reported that the peaks and troughs in prices and development activities, measured by the number of oil and gas wells drilled, largely overlapped, strongly suggesting that development activities reacted quickly and proportionally to changes in the prices of oil and gas.

- *Increased development of shale oil and shale gas.* BLM officials and industry representatives cited the growth in development of oil and natural gas from shale formations (shale oil and shale gas) as a significant change in the oil and gas sector that has influenced where oil and gas resources are developed. This growth was made possible in part due to technological advancements in combining horizontal drilling techniques and hydraulic fracturing. According to BLM officials and industry representatives, the increase in the development of shale oil and shale gas has largely occurred on state and private lands. This is consistent with our finding from September 2012, when we reported that the location of shale formations appears to be predominately on nonfederal lands, according to an official from the Energy Information Administration.[22] Also, an oil and gas industry representative we interviewed said the economics have become more attractive for developing oil and gas from shale formations than from other onshore sources. For example, the industry representative said that shale gas wells have, in general, become more profitable than coalbed methane wells in recent years. This is due in part to the fact that shale gas

---

[21]GAO, *Onshore Oil and Gas: BLM's Management of Public Protests to Its Lease Sales Needs Improvement*, GAO-10-670 (Washington, D.C.: July 30, 2010).

[22]GAO-12-732.

wells often produce more natural gas than coalbed methane wells and also because coalbed methane wells generally involve additional costs associated with the disposal of large quantities of water they produce.

- *Differences between federal and state permitting processes.* Oil and gas industry representatives said there is a perception in the industry that the permitting process and regulatory environment associated with developing federal oil and gas resources is more complex and time-consuming than for oil and gas resources located on state or private lands. According to these representatives, delays in obtaining permits are costly for operators and may prompt operators to seek to develop oil and gas on state and private lands rather than on federal lands. BLM officials said that BLM must consider multiple uses of the land and that the environmental standards and legal requirements they must follow when managing oil and gas development may differ from the requirements for state or private lands.

APD Activity Has Varied by Location

Permitting activity since 2007 has varied among BLM offices, as shown in table 1. For instance, 23 of BLM's 33 lead oil and gas offices received fewer APDs for federal oil and gas resources in fiscal year 2012 than in fiscal year 2007; 9 offices received more APDs; and 1 office did not experience any change in APDs received.

Table 1: Change in the Number of Applications for Permit to Drill Received by BLM Offices from Fiscal Years 2007 to 2012

Office name (state)	Number of APDs received (FY 07)	Number of APDs received (FY 12)	Change in number of APDs received (FY 07 to FY 12)
Buffalo FO (WY)	2,673	127	-2,546
Farmington FO (NM)	825	96	-729
Pinedale FO (WY)	814	326	-488
Rawlins FO (WY)	372	126	-246
Colorado River Valley FO (CO)	383	182	-201
Great Falls Oil and Gas FO (MT)	103	1	-102
White River FO (CO)	199	106	-93
Miles City FO (MT)	122	43	-79
Rock Springs FO (WY)	149	73	-76
Kemmerer FO (WY)	87	16	-71

Office name (state)	Number of APDs received (FY 07)	Number of APDs received (FY 12)	Change in number of APDs received (FY 07 to FY 12)
Southeastern States FO (MS)	93	24	-69
Roswell FO (NM)	68	7	-61
Lander FO (WY)	81	24	-57
Worland FO (WY)	78	22	-56
Royal Gorge FO (CO)	81	30	-51
Moab FO (UT)	56	13	-43
Tres Rios FO (CO)	41	10	-31
Little Snake FO (CO)	50	21	-29
Northeastern States FO (WI)	16	1	-15
Salt Lake FO (UT)	9	0	-9
Nevada State Office (NV)	17	10	-7
Rio Puerco FO (NM)	9	5	-4
Alaska State Office (AK)	4	2	-2
Newcastle FO (WY)	52	52	0
Grand Junction FO (CO)	48	49	1
Bakersfield FO (CA)	279	287	8
Price FO (UT)	77	92	15
Oklahoma FO (OK)	48	79	31
Casper FO (WY)	90	158	68
Vernal FO (UT)	946	1072	126
Hobbs Field Station (NM)	145	283	138
North Dakota FO (ND)	84	287	203
Carlsbad FO (NM)	474	679	205
Total	**8,573**	**4,303**	**-4,270**

Legend: FY = fiscal year; FO = Field Office.

Source: GAO analysis of BLM data.

Note: The names of offices participating in the Federal Permit Streamlining Pilot Project, which was established in section 365 of the Energy Policy Act of 2005 to improve oil and gas permitting, are presented in bold. This table presents data on applications for permit to drill (APD) for federal oil and gas resources and does not include APDs received by BLM for nonfederal oil and gas resources on Indian Trust lands. According to BLM officials, APDs for nonfederal oil and gas resources on Indian Trust lands are a sizeable portion of some BLM offices' permitting workload.

Variations in the level of permitting activity in different locations from fiscal year 2007 to fiscal year 2012 reflect the general shift in the types of APDs submitted to BLM that occurred over the same time period. For example, in fiscal year 2007, the Buffalo Field Office in Wyoming received more APDs than any other office, and nearly 98 percent of the APDs received were for coalbed methane wells. However, as the number of APDs for

GAO-13-572 BLM Oil and Gas Development

coalbed methane has declined in recent years, the Buffalo Field Office has experienced a significant drop in the number of new APDs it received, declining from 2,673 APDs in fiscal year 2007 down to 127 APDs in fiscal year 2012. As a result of this decline, the Buffalo Field Office transitioned from receiving more than 30 percent of all APDs for federal oil and gas resources in fiscal year 2007 to receiving about 3 percent of all APDs by fiscal year 2012.[23]

In contrast, BLM's North Dakota Field Office experienced more than a 240 percent increase in the number of APDs it received, from 84 in fiscal year 2007 to 287 in fiscal year 2012, and all of the APDs were for oil wells.[24] The North Dakota Field Office, which was the seventeenth most active BLM office for APDs received in fiscal year 2007, ranked as the fourth most active BLM office in fiscal year 2012.[25] In response to the increase in APDs at the North Dakota Field Office, BLM officials said the agency created two special response strike teams in 2012 that consisted of 10 to 12 oil and gas staff from field offices across BLM. These teams helped process pending APDs for about 3 weeks and, according to BLM officials, the strike teams assisted in approving more than 200 APDs for federal and Indian Trust wells. BLM officials also said that they may consider using the strike team concept again under certain circumstances, such as when a field office experiences a large increase in APDs.

---

[23]The Buffalo Field Office is responsible for managing the second largest number of federal oil and gas wells of all BLM offices (see fig. 1 in the Background of this report). In fiscal year 2012, this office accounted for 10 of the 19 (about 53 percent) coalbed methane APDs received by BLM.

[24]These numbers represent APDs for federal oil and gas resources that the North Dakota Field Office received. According to BLM officials, Indian Trust APDs represent a significant part of the North Dakota Field Office's overall permitting workload, but those APDs were not included in our analysis.

[25]The North Dakota Field Office was tied with the Bakersfield Field Office for the fourth most active BLM office in terms of APDs for federal oil and gas resources received in fiscal year 2012.

BLM Has Taken Actions to Better Manage Its Oil and Gas Permitting Workload, but Challenges Remain

BLM has taken actions to improve its management of its oil and gas permitting workload since we last reported on this issue in 2005, including revising its permitting rule in 2007, developing plans for a new APD processing system, and implementing a pilot project that increased funding and staff for APD processing. Even with the actions taken to address its permitting workload, BLM continues to face challenges with APD processing.

BLM Revised Its Permitting Rule, Developed Plans for a New APD Processing System, and Implemented a Pilot Permitting Project

Since we reported on BLM's oil and gas permitting workload in 2005, BLM has implemented a number of actions to manage its changing permitting workload and implement provisions of the Energy Policy Act of 2005. These actions include (1) revising its oil and gas permitting rule, (2) developing plans for a new APD processing system, and (3) implementing a pilot project in some field offices to streamline APD processing. The impact of some of these actions on BLM's performance and effectiveness is not yet known because BLM has not completed fully implemented or fully evaluated the actions.

Revisions to BLM's Permitting Rule

In March 2007, BLM issued its revised rule for oil and gas permitting, known as Onshore Oil and Gas Order Number 1 (the order), which specifies the requirements necessary for the approval of proposed oil and gas wells on areas covered by federal onshore oil and gas leases.[26] The order incorporated changes in law, policy, procedures, and requirements that had been implemented since the previous rule for oil and gas permitting was published in 1983. These changes include the Federal Onshore Oil and Gas Leasing Reform Act of 1987 and the Energy Policy Act of 2005. The order includes several changes that could affect BLM's permitting workload, the content of the APDs submitted by operators, and the procedures BLM uses to process those APDs. Among other things, the order:

[26]72 Fed. Reg. 10,308 (March 7, 2007).

- Clarified what operators must include in an APD for it to be considered complete.[27] Key components include (1) a completed application form, (2) a well plat depicting the proposed location and boundaries of the proposed development, (3) a Drilling Plan containing technical information such as the operator's minimum specifications for blowout prevention equipment, (4) a Surface Use Plan of Operations, (5) evidence of bond coverage,[28] and (6) operator certification that the information it has provided in the APD is correct and that the operator will develop the proposed site in conformity with the terms and conditions of the APD.

- Incorporated the required deadlines for APD processing established by the Energy Policy Act of 2005 which, among other things, requires BLM to (1) notify the operator within 10 days of receiving an APD as to whether or not the APD is complete and (2) approve or defer the APD within 30 days after the operator has submitted a complete APD.[29]

- Established a new approval process for Master Development Plans, which allows operators to submit multiple APDs together for wells that share a common Drilling Plan and Surface Use Plan of Operations. According to BLM officials, a Master Development Plan increases processing efficiency and enables BLM to consider the cumulative effects of development early in the process of developing an oil and gas field to minimize adverse environmental impacts.

- Encouraged operators to voluntarily use environmental best management practices when developing their APDs and stated that BLM may incorporate these practices as required COAs based on the

---

[27]Before an APD is considered complete, BLM must also perform an on-site inspection of the proposed well site to help determine if the materials submitted in the APD package are accurate and whether any COAs are necessary. The operator must correct any deficiencies identified during this on-site inspection. The on-site inspections that occur during the permitting phase are not included in our analysis of BLM's environmental inspection activities.

[28]These bonds are intended to ensure that operators perform the required reclamation, as well as the lease's other terms and conditions, such as the payment of federal royalties.

[29]The order also provides that, under certain conditions, BLM may deny an APD within 30 days.

GAO-13-572 BLM Oil and Gas Development

results of the NEPA analysis or other analyses performed during the APD review process.[30]

Development and Planned Implementation of a New APD Processing and Tracking System

In 2012, BLM announced plans to implement a new automated APD processing and tracking system in 2013. According to information provided by BLM, this new system is intended to help BLM process APDs faster and more efficiently and improve the quality of data on APDs tracked by the agency. Specifically, the new system is expected to improve APD processing and data quality by:

- Promoting the use of online submissions of APDs and automatically preventing the submission of an APD if any required fields are incomplete. Currently, operators can submit APDs to BLM in hard copy format or electronically. According to information provided by BLM, operators will be able to input APD data directly into BLM's new system and will be automatically alerted if any information is missing.

- Improving BLM's workflow by automatically generating the letters BLM sends to operators about their APDs and the results of BLM's review process, thus reducing the time it takes staff to prepare these letters. Also, according to BLM officials, the new system will improve the routing of different parts of the APD package to various BLM specialists (e.g., petroleum engineers or geologists) for their review.

- Allowing operators to electronically track the progress of their submitted APDs and identify delays so that they can proactively resolve issues with BLM. Under current practice, operators must either wait for BLM to contact them about problems with APDs or contact staff in BLM offices to identify any deficiencies that need resolution.

- Allowing BLM to better track and evaluate its progress in processing APDs and to identify common sources of delays. According to BLM officials, the new system will support more advanced analyses of BLM's processing performance and improve the quality of BLM's data by, for example, automatically recording some dates associated with the processing of APDs.

---

[30]As we reported in June 2005, BLM established its agency policy on the use of environmental best management practices in 2004, but officials from some field offices said they had already been using these practices prior to the issuance of the agency policy. See GAO-05-418.

According to BLM officials, a similar APD processing and tracking system used by the Carlsbad Field Office since 2007 has helped reduce the time it takes to process APDs in that office. BLM officials said they expect to implement the new APD processing and tracking system agency-wide within calendar year 2013. According to BLM officials, the new APD processing and tracking system is one step in a broader effort to upgrade its oil and gas IT systems and replace AFMSS in the future.

BLM Implemented a Pilot Project to Streamline Permit Processing

As prescribed by section 365 of the Energy Policy Act of 2005, BLM implemented the Federal Permit Streamlining Pilot Project. According to a Memorandum of Understanding signed by the Departments of Agriculture, the Army, and the Interior, as well as the Environmental Protection Agency, the project was aimed at improving the processing of APDs and coordination among BLM and other federal and state agencies on oil and gas permitting issues. The Energy Policy Act of 2005 required the Secretary of the Interior to increase staff in seven BLM field offices as necessary to ensure the effective implementation of the Pilot Project and other programs administered by the field offices, such as their oil and gas inspection and enforcement programs. The seven pilot offices are Rawlins and Buffalo, Wyoming; Miles City, Montana; Farmington and Carlsbad, New Mexico; Grand Junction/Glenwood Springs, Colorado (now called the Colorado River Valley Field Office); and Vernal, Utah.

To help implement the Pilot Project, the Energy Policy Act of 2005 established a Permit Processing Improvement Fund to provide funds that BLM can use or transfer to other agencies, such as Interior's Fish and Wildlife Service. With some of these funds, BLM hired additional staff to assist with APD processing and inspection and enforcement efforts in the seven pilot offices. According to a 2008 report assessing the Pilot Project that was prepared for BLM, the agency had hired more than 140 new staff members for the seven pilot offices by the end of fiscal year 2007.[31] This report assessed the overall impact and results of the Pilot Project in its first 2 years of implementation—fiscal years 2006 and 2007—and analyzed a variety of performance measures established by BLM for the project, including APD workloads and the average number of days it took the pilot offices to process APDs from date of receipt to date of approval.

[31]Booz Allen Hamilton, *Section 365 of the Energy Policy Act of 2005: Year Two Report for the Pilot Project to Improve Federal Permit Coordination*, a report prepared for the Department of the Interior's Bureau of Land Management (Washington, D.C.: February 2008).

GAO-13-572 BLM Oil and Gas Development

According to the report, the total number of APDs processed by the seven pilot offices increased by more than 10 percent from fiscal year 2005 (the year before the Pilot Project began) to fiscal year 2007, but the average number of days it took to process the APDs from date of receipt to date of approval increased by more than 40 percent during the same period.

The Energy Policy Act of 2005 required Interior to issue a report to Congress by August 2008 that outlined the results of the Pilot Project to date and also make a recommendation to the President on whether the Pilot Project should be implemented throughout the United States, such as by expanding to all field offices. BLM, however, has not met this requirement. The 2008 assessment covered fiscal years 2006 and 2007, but it did not contain a recommendation on the future of the Pilot Project. Instead, the report stated that BLM would issue a separate report that would outline the results of the project and make a recommendation on whether it should be implemented in BLM's nonpilot offices as well. BLM officials prepared a draft report dated August 2009 but, as of April 2013, BLM officials said there was no date set for its completion. As of June 2013, this report had not been finalized or released. The 2009 draft report contained an analysis of the results of the Pilot Project through fiscal year 2008 and also included recommendations.[32] According to a BLM official, the report was not finalized or cleared by Interior or the Office of Management and Budget and therefore was not submitted to Congress. We asked BLM for supporting documentation of why the report was not finalized or submitted to Congress, but BLM did not provide any additional information.

Since BLM has not completed an assessment of the Pilot Project since 2008, it is unclear whether the project has met its goals or whether changes would improve its performance and effectiveness. Nevertheless, in its fiscal year 2014 budget request, BLM proposed changes to the Pilot Project and the Permit Processing Improvement Fund portion of the Pilot Project. Specifically, BLM is seeking flexibility to change which of its offices are pilot offices as needed based on changing permitting demands. BLM has also proposed that Congress eliminate the Permit Processing Improvement Fund and the annual APD fees beginning in 2015 and replace them by authorizing BLM to establish cost recovery

---

[32]In a letter transmitting the draft report to us, BLM indicated the report contains outdated information, including obsolete budgetary and legislative information, and does not represent departmental policy.

fees for APDs that would finance BLM's labor and other expenses in processing the APDs. As of May 2013, Congress had not acted on these proposals. We asked for more details about how the proposed changes in funding would affect BLM's ability to carry out its operations under the Pilot Project, but BLM did not provide additional information, such as the amount of funds anticipated to be generated by the proposed change compared with the funds BLM is currently receiving. Instead, BLM officials said that the amount of funding BLM would receive through the APD cost recovery fees would vary based on the number of APDs submitted in a given year and thus may be subject to peaks and valleys based on fluctuations in permitting levels. It is uncertain what impact these or other changes would have on the Pilot Project and BLM's ability to process APDs.

BLM Faces Challenges Meeting and Assessing Its Compliance with the Required Processing Deadline for Completed APDs and Does Not Consistently Track Key APD Data

In a 2013 internal memorandum, BLM reported that it had not been able to meet the 30-day deadline required by the Energy Policy Act of 2005 to process (either approve or defer) completed APDs, and that it has struggled to consistently track the amount of time it takes to process APDs due to data gaps in AFMSS. Specifically, BLM reported that the APD data in AFMSS were incomplete and missing critical processing dates, making it difficult to reliably track and make adjustments to any steps in the APD review process to improve its operations.

Similarly, our analysis of BLM's APD data from fiscal years 2007 to 2012 identified challenges with the completeness and accuracy of the data on APDs' completion dates. We found that the data in AFMSS were missing completion dates for some APDs and contained potential inaccurate entries for the completion dates for other APDs. An APD's completion date is important because it is needed to determine whether BLM complied with the required 30-day deadline to approve or defer completed APDs, and because it helps BLM track how much time is spent in the two periods of the APD review process—Period 1, which is the time from initial submission of an APD until the time BLM determines an APD is complete, and Period 2, which is the time from when an APD is designated as complete until the time BLM makes a decision to approve, or in limited instances deny, the completed APD. Without accurate data on the amount of time spent in each period, it is difficult to determine whether any actions could be taken to improve the efficiency of the APD review process. Figure 4 depicts the steps that occur in each period of the review process, as well as key dates and requirements, including the requirement for BLM to approve or defer completed APDs within 30 days.

Figure 4: Overview of Selected Key Dates, Steps, and Requirements in BLM's Review Process for Applications for Permit to Drill

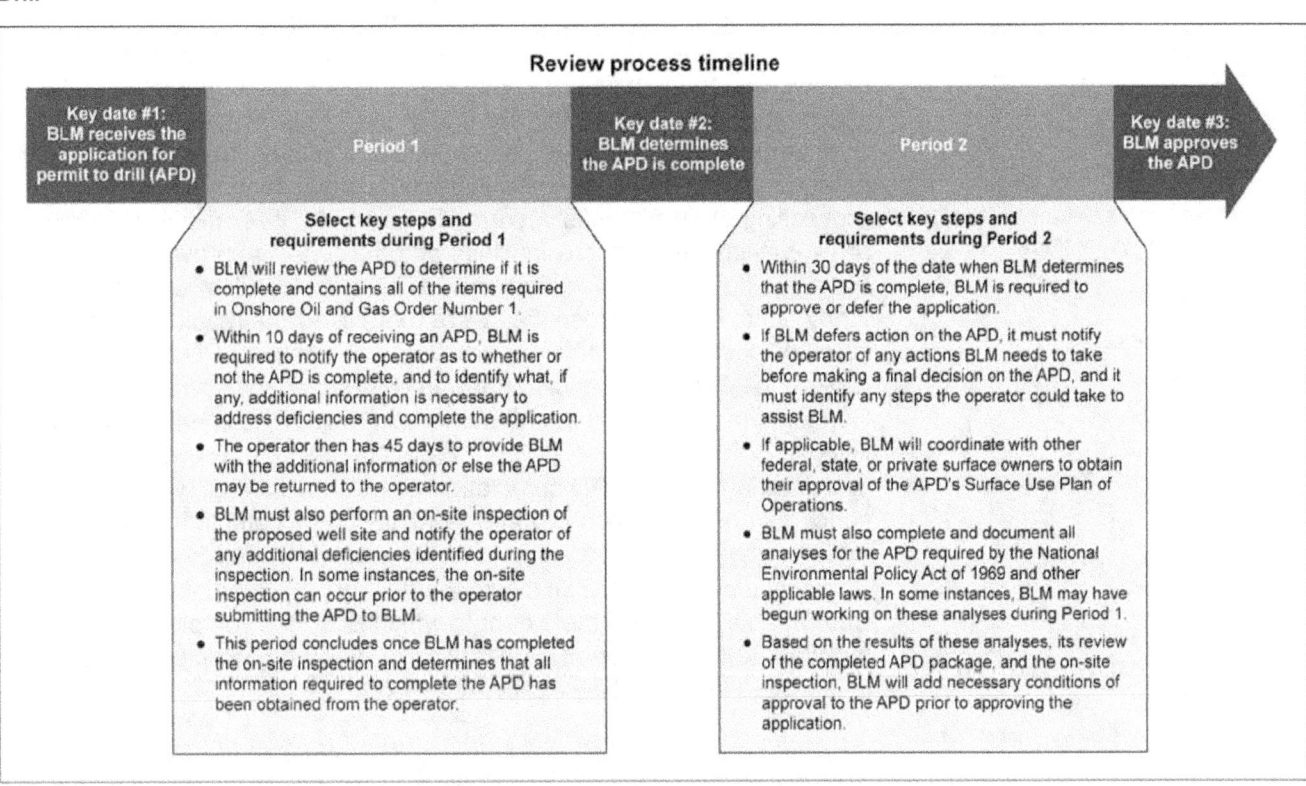

Source: GAO analysis of BLM documents and information.

Note: This figure focuses on the review process for APDs that are approved by BLM, but in limited instances BLM may also deny APDs if its review finds there are no actions the operator could take that would enable BLM to issue the permit. The steps described in this figure apply to APDs for all well types, including oil, natural gas, and coalbed methane wells.

We reviewed BLM's data on nearly 27,400 APDs approved from fiscal year 2007 to fiscal year 2012 and found that approximately 5,160 (about 19 percent) of the APDs did not have a completion date entered in AFMSS.[33] Furthermore, even when the APD data we reviewed included a

---

[33]The nearly 27,400 approved APDs for which we reviewed data represented approximately 89 percent of all APDs for federal oil and gas resources that BLM has reported it approved from fiscal years 2007 to 2012. We were unable to obtain sufficient data on the remaining 11 percent of APDs that BLM has reported it approved during this time period to include them in our analysis.

completion date, we identified differences among BLM offices in how the data were entered; this suggests that inaccurate completion dates may have been recorded for some APDs. In particular, the data on more than 5,560 of the nearly 27,400 approved APDs (about 20 percent) we reviewed listed the same date for when the APD was completed as for its approval. In other words, the data for these APDs indicate that it took BLM zero additional days to process the APDs once the agency determined the APDs were complete, thus suggesting the entire processing of these APDs occurred in Period 1. BLM officials said there are some limited instances in which an office could approve an APD on the same day that it was determined to be complete. However, they said many of the cases we identified were more likely the result of staff from some offices following different practices for entering APD completion dates into AFMSS and misinterpreting BLM's guidance on this matter. Consequently, we cannot confirm the accuracy of the completion dates listed in AFMSS for these APDs.[34] Also, because of these different practices in entering APD completion dates into AFMSS, we have concerns about the accuracy and reliability of the completion dates listed for the remaining 61 percent of the APDs for which we reviewed data.[35] As a result of these problems with the data on APD completion dates, we were unable to assess the extent to which BLM has complied with the required 30-day deadline for approving or deferring completed APDs established in the Energy Policy Act of 2005.

On April 15, 2013, BLM issued new guidance on APD processing and data entry that states, among other things, that BLM staff are required to enter the APD completion date into AFMSS and clarifies how BLM staff should determine this date. BLM officials said they expect the new guidance to help improve the reliability of BLM's APD data.

We also analyzed BLM data on approved APDs to assess the average number of days it took BLM to process APDs from date of receipt to date

[34]Our concern about the reliability of the data on these 5,160 APDs is focused on their listed completion date in AFMSS and does not extend to their received and approved dates listed in the database. Consequently, we included these APDs in our analysis of data on the average number of days it took BLM to process APDs from date of receipt to date of approval discussed below.

[35]As a result of the concerns about the reliability of the listed completion dates for these APDs, we were unable to quantify how much of the processing time for these APDs was spent in each of the two review periods.

of approval, and the extent to which this may have changed from fiscal year 2007 to fiscal year 2012. We found that the number of days from date of receipt to date of approval averaged 229 days in fiscal year 2012. However, due to the incompleteness of data in AFMSS, we were unable to determine how this average changed from fiscal year 2007 to fiscal year 2012. Without information on how the average number of days has changed, it is difficult to determine whether actions could be taken to improve BLM's APD review process. Specifically, we were unable to obtain data on the approval date for APDs that BLM reported were approved during fiscal years 2007 to 2012 but later had expired or were rescinded, cancelled, or withdrawn without a well having been drilled. Once an APD has expired or been rescinded, cancelled, or withdrawn, AFMSS stops retaining data on the approval date for that APD. Since approved APDs can potentially remain valid for up to 4 years, APDs approved in the earlier years of the period we analyzed were more likely to have expired and be missing an approval date than APDs that were approved more recently. For example, the data we obtained from AFMSS did not include the approval dates for about 23 percent of the APDs that BLM reported were approved in fiscal year 2007. In contrast, less than 1 percent of the APDs that BLM reported were approved in fiscal year 2012 were missing approval dates.[36] Further, BLM officials confirmed that they also cannot accurately determine how the average number of days to process APDs from date of receipt to date of approval has changed over time for individual offices due to the problem of approval dates not being retained in AFMSS for APDs that have expired or have been rescinded, cancelled, or withdrawn. According to BLM officials, BLM intends to address this problem with data retention as it replaces AFMSS in the future. BLM officials did not estimate when changes to improve the tracking of APD approval dates would occur, but they did not expect this change to be part of the new APD processing and tracking system that is expected to be implemented within calendar year 2013.

BLM officials and industry representatives we interviewed identified a variety of factors that may contribute to the amount of time it takes BLM to

---

[36]The data we obtained from BLM on APDs approved in fiscal years 2009 to 2011 were more complete than the data from fiscal years 2007 and 2008 but were less complete in some years than the data from fiscal year 2012. As a result of the variation in the completeness of the data on APDs approved from fiscal years 2007 to 2012 and uncertainty about the impact of the missing data, we limited our reporting of the average number of days to process an APD from date of receipt to date of approval to fiscal year 2012.

process an APD from its date of receipt to its date of approval. For example, BLM officials we spoke with identified several factors, including:

- *The level of complexity of the APDs being submitted by operators.* In its 2014 budget justification report, BLM reported that the time it takes to process APDs has increased or remained high due to the increased complexity of issues analyzed in environmental documents associated with new APDs.[37] According to BLM officials, some of the new areas being developed may have unique challenges that are encountered during the permitting phase, such as operators seeking to drill in new locations that involve more challenging terrain or habitat for sensitive species, which can increase the complexity of the APDs.

- *The use of Master Development Plans.* BLM officials said that Master Development Plans—in which operators submit multiple APDs together that share a common Drilling Plan and Surface Use Plan of Operations—are beneficial for the environment because they allow BLM to assess the cumulative environmental impacts of proposed development on a project-level scale rather than on a well-by-well basis. However, officials said it generally takes BLM more time to process these plans given their larger scope. According to BLM officials, AFMSS does not currently track whether an APD was approved as part of a Master Development Plan, but this information will be tracked under the new APD processing and tracking system once it has been implemented.

- *Operators submitting incomplete APDs and taking longer to correct deficiencies.* In its 2014 budget justification report, BLM reported that due to turnover in operators' permitting staff, the agency often receives inconsistent and incomplete APDs. BLM reported this has contributed to longer times to process APDs. According to BLM officials, since an operator's new employees may not be familiar with the APD process and BLM's requirements, they may be more likely to submit incomplete APDs and take longer to correct deficiencies.

- *The use of categorical exclusions.* BLM officials also said it is possible that changes in how frequently categorical exclusions are used to approve oil and gas APDs could influence the amount of time it takes

---

[37]Department of the Interior, *Budget Justifications and Performance Information Fiscal Year 2014: Bureau of Land Management* (Washington, D.C.: 2013).

BLM to process APDs.[38] The Energy Policy Act of 2005 established several categorical exclusions under which, if conditions are met, BLM need not prepare any new environmental impact analysis, such as an environmental assessment or environmental impact statement, which would ordinarily be required for oil and gas projects. However, since, according to BLM officials, the agency has not maintained data on the use of categorical exclusions in recent years, it is unclear to what extent this issue has impacted the amount of time it took BLM to process APDs since 2007.

Industry representatives we interviewed also cited the level of complexity of an APD as one factor that contributes to the amount of time it takes BLM to process an APD from date of receipt to date of approval. However, industry representatives cited other factors specific to BLM that could affect the time it takes to process APDs. For example, industry representatives stated that, in their experience, the amount of time it takes BLM to process APDs is noticeably longer in some offices than in others. They attributed the differences to inadequate BLM staffing in some offices with large APD workloads, inconsistent standards for processing APDs, and their opinion that some BLM offices place less urgency on processing APDs than other offices do. Industry representatives we spoke with also said that the amount of time it takes BLM to process APDs may make the development of federal oil and gas resources less attractive to oil and gas operators in some situations.

---

[38]Under certain circumstances established in section 390 of the Energy Policy Act of 2005, BLM can approve an APD relying on a categorical exclusion rather than preparing the environmental impact statement or environmental assessment that is normally required under NEPA for an APD. See GAO, *Energy Policy Act of 2005: BLM's Use of Section 390 Categorical Exclusions for Oil and Gas Development,* GAO-11-941T (Washington, D.C.: Sept. 9, 2011).

BLM Has Taken Actions to Better Mitigate the Environmental Impact of Oil and Gas Development, but Challenges Remain

To mitigate the environmental impact of oil and gas development, BLM has increased the number of environmental inspections completed on federal oil and gas wells and facilities from fiscal year 2007 to fiscal year 2012. Nevertheless, BLM continues to face challenges in mitigating the environmental impact of oil and gas development due to insufficient information and inconsistent documentation of its inspection and enforcement actions and staffing challenges.

BLM Has Increased the Number of Environmental Inspections to Better Mitigate the Environmental Impact of Oil and Gas Development

BLM increased the number of environmental inspections it performed on federal oil and gas wells and facilities by approximately 63 percent, from 10,941 in fiscal year 2007 to 17,866 in fiscal year 2012. The number of environmental inspections performed in fiscal year 2012 was about 1 percent lower than the peak reached in fiscal year 2011, when BLM performed 18,110 environmental inspections.[39] Table 2 shows the change in environmental inspections from fiscal year 2007 to fiscal year 2012 among BLM offices.

Table 2: Change in the Number of Environmental Inspections Performed by BLM Offices from Fiscal Years 2007 to 2012

Office name (state)	Number of environmental inspections (FY 07)	Number of environmental inspections (FY 12)	Change in number of environmental inspections (FY 07 to FY 12)
Pinedale FO (WY)	604	2,320	1,716
Buffalo FO (WY)	1,826	3,461	1,635
Vernal FO (UT)	318	1,752	1,434
Colorado River Valley FO (CO)	376	1,417	1,041
Farmington FO (NM)	386	965	579
Carlsbad FO (NM)	1,104	1,590	486
White River FO (CO)	48	402	354

[39]Prior to the slight decline in fiscal year 2012, BLM had increased the number of environmental inspections it performed on federal oil and gas wells and facilities every year from fiscal year 2007 to fiscal year 2011.

Office name (state)	Number of environmental inspections (FY 07)	Number of environmental inspections (FY 12)	Change in number of environmental inspections (FY 07 to FY 12)
Kemmerer FO (WY)	36	376	340
Great Falls Oil and Gas FO (MT)	108	438	330
Bakersfield FO (CA)	232	503	271
Newcastle FO (WY)	3	211	208
Oklahoma FO (OK)	47	187	140
Alaska State Office (AK)	12	116	104
Lander FO (WY)	4	104	100
Tres Rios FO (CO)	57	151	94
Northeastern States FO (WI)	162	250	88
Moab FO (UT)	26	99	73
Salt Lake FO (UT)	0	27	27
Casper FO (WY)	107	120	13
Price FO (UT)	98	102	4
Rawlins FO (WY)	514	491	-23
Royal Gorge FO (CO)	55	24	-31
Miles City FO (MT)	361	329	-32
Rio Puerco FO (NM)	52	19	-33
Hobbs Field Station (NM)	867	833	-34
North Dakota FO (ND)	239	192	-47
Nevada State Office (NV)	87	15	-72
Southeastern States FO (MS)	247	142	-105
Little Snake FO (CO)	247	92	-155
Grand Junction FO (CO)	361	175	-186
Rock Springs FO (WY)	779	392	-387
Roswell FO (NM)	664	171	-493
Worland FO (WY)	914	400	-514
Total	**10,941**	**17,866**	**6,925**

Legend: FY = fiscal year; FO = Field Office.

Source: GAO analysis of BLM data.

Note: This table presents data on environmental inspection performed on federal oil and gas wells and facilities and does not include information on environmental inspections performed by BLM on nonfederal oil and gas wells or facilities located on Indian Trust lands. In addition, the table excludes results from more than 580 environmental inspections recorded in BLM's Automated Fluid Minerals Support System database in fiscal year 2012 and more than 160 environmental inspections recorded in fiscal year 2007 due to concerns about the accuracy of the data. The names of offices participating in the Federal Permit Streamlining Pilot Project, which was established in section 365 of the Energy Policy Act of 2005 to improve oil and gas permitting, are in bold.

BLM offices with the greatest increases in environmental inspections from fiscal year 2007 to fiscal year 2012 were generally those responsible for managing the most federal oil and gas wells. The three offices with the greatest increase in environmental inspections from fiscal year 2007 to fiscal year 2012 were the Pinedale and Buffalo Field Offices in Wyoming, and the Vernal Field Office, in Utah. As of December 2012, these three offices also managed nearly 27 percent of all federal oil and gas wells. Similarly, BLM's Farmington Field Office, in New Mexico, managed the largest number of federal wells as of December 2012 and increased the environmental inspections it performed, from 386 in fiscal year 2007 to 965 in fiscal year 2012.

BLM management officials at three field offices said that having fewer APDs to process has allowed their environmental staff, who also help process APDs, to spend more time on enforcement activities, including environmental inspections. For example, the number of APDs received by the Pinedale Field Office dropped from 814 in fiscal year 2007 to 326 in fiscal year 2012, and the number of environmental inspections it performed increased from 604 to 2,320 during that period. In contrast, some offices that experienced an increase in APDs during the period conducted fewer environmental inspections. For example, the North Dakota Field Office, which experienced a 240 percent increase in the number of APDs received from fiscal years 2007 to 2012, going from 84 APDs in fiscal year 2007 to 287 APDs in fiscal year 2012, performed nearly 20 percent fewer environmental inspections during the same period, going from 239 environmental inspections in fiscal year 2007 to 192 in fiscal year 2012.

BLM officials attributed the overall increase in environmental inspections to the following actions:

- BLM revised its guidance for documenting environmental inspection activities, particularly interim reclamation inspections. In 2005, we recommended that BLM track interim reclamation inspections in its centralized database.[40] In response, BLM required field office staff to enter those data into AFMSS. BLM also developed a new inspection form to ensure that data gathered during reclamation inspections were standardized. These actions improved tracking of BLM's environmental inspection workload, according to BLM officials.

- BLM increased the focus on environmental inspections by establishing targets for managers and staff and including those targets in annual staff performance plans and expectations. For example, metrics are included in the annual performance plans for certain BLM state directors who oversee offices involved in oil and gas development. These metrics generally specify that the state directors should ensure that their offices conduct all high-priority environmental inspections identified during the inspection prioritization process. Also, BLM field office management staff said that their annual performance plans include meeting their office's high-priority environmental inspections targets. In addition, environmental staff said that they had targets for the number of environmental inspections they were expected to complete in a given fiscal year.

- BLM increased environmental inspections as a result of the Pilot Project that enabled some field offices to hire additional staff and designate some environmental staff to work primarily on environmental inspections. At the four pilot offices we contacted,[41] some environmental staff reported working only on environmental inspections. In contrast, staff at other field offices we visited reported that environmental staff usually conduct environmental inspections and process APDs.

- BLM field offices increased the planned amount of work time devoted to environmental inspections. In fiscal year 2007, BLM offices reported planning to spend about 131 workmonths (a workmonth is about 172 hours) on environmental inspections. In fiscal year 2012,

---

[40]GAO-05-418.

[41]The pilot offices we contacted were Colorado River Valley in Colorado, Carlsbad and Farmington in New Mexico, and Vernal in Utah.

BLM offices planned to spend 182 workmonths on environmental inspections.[42]

- In some cases, environmental staff can perform more inspections due to efficiencies created when the average number of wells per well pad increases, and when new wells are drilled in closer proximity to other wells, according to BLM officials. Some field offices reported that technology such as directional drilling has enabled operators to place more wells on a given well pad. This allows BLM inspectors to review more wells in a given time frame.[43]

BLM's Environmental Mitigation Efforts Are Hampered by Insufficient Information, Inconsistent Documentation, and Staffing Challenges

BLM's environmental mitigation efforts are hampered by (1) an environmental inspection prioritization process that does not have sufficient information to ensure that wells receiving inspections are those that pose the greatest environmental risk, (2) inconsistent documentation of inspections and enforcement actions, and (3) challenges with retaining and hiring environmental staff in some offices.

BLM's Inspection Prioritization Process Does Not Have Information to Ensure Wells Receiving Inspections Pose Greatest Environmental Risk

BLM's environmental inspection prioritization process does not effectively ensure that the wells posing the greatest environment risk are identified as high-priority for environmental inspections conducted each year. In particular, BLM staff face challenges obtaining information from AFMSS to prioritize wells for environmental inspections, and BLM staff do not have sufficient information on the environmental condition of wells that have never received an environmental inspection.

Environmental staff in some BLM field offices reported challenges using AFMSS to identify which wells should be considered high-priority for environmental inspections each year because AFMSS does not have the capability to flag individual wells as high priority for environmental concerns. Consequently, some BLM environmental staff said that they must rely on their own knowledge and memory of wells to determine which ones meet prioritization criteria. Also, some environmental staff

---

[42]We did not analyze the extent to which the actual number of workmonths BLM spent on environmental inspections for these years matched or differed from the number of planned environmental inspection workmonths recorded in BLM's planning documents.

[43]BLM officials noted that the placing of more wells on a given pad reduces habitat fragmentation (the breaking up a large area of habitat into smaller areas) and thus provides additional benefits to wildlife.

said they sometimes selected wells to inspect based on convenience, including selecting some that were close to each other. BLM officials said that the agency is planning to replace AFMSS with a new system that, among other things, can be used by staff to prioritize and develop targets for environmental inspections. However, the officials said that due to budget uncertainties they could not say when this will occur.

BLM also does not have information on the environmental condition of many wells. We analyzed data on approximately 60,330 federal oil and gas wells on lands managed by BLM and found no record for about 24,840, or 41 percent, in AFMSS of those wells ever having received an environmental inspection as of December 2012. At least 75 percent of the wells with no environmental inspection record in AFMSS became capable of production in fiscal year 2007 or earlier. Since there is no environmental inspection history for these wells in AFMSS, BLM does not have the information to assess whether the wells pose any current environmental risks or whether sufficient environmental mitigation has occurred. BLM environmental staff said that wells with no record of an environmental inspection could have environmental problems that go undetected.

According to BLM officials, it is possible that some of these wells may have been inspected for environmental issues, but that the inspections were not recorded in AFMSS. Nevertheless, it would still be difficult for BLM staff attempting to prioritize environmental inspections to determine the environmental condition of wells under these circumstances, since the information on their previous environmental inspections is not in AFMSS. For example, BLM officials said some environmental inspections of federal oil and gas wells performed in fiscal years 2005 and 2006 were likely never entered into AFMSS because the database was shut down for several months in 2005 as a result of a court order. BLM officials also said that it is possible that some wells could have been inspected prior to the development of AFMSS in 1997, and that information was not entered into AFMSS. In addition, BLM officials said that when ownership of an oil and gas lease on federal lands changes through sale, trade, or transfer, AFMSS deletes certain inspection dates.

BLM officials also said that some of the wells we identified with no record of an environmental inspection in AFMSS may have received other types of inspections, such as production inspections, that would have identified any significant environmental issues. We did not determine whether the wells we identified as having no environmental inspection records had received other types of inspections. However, in 2011, a BLM internal assessment of inspection and enforcement activities in several field offices found examples of wells that had not received an inspection of any kind despite being in production for 10 to 12 years.[44] Furthermore, according to BLM officials, the other types of inspections would typically be conducted by staff who do not have the same training as the environmental inspection staff. For example, environmental staff are generally trained in such areas as interim reclamation and environmental best management practices and can assess the adequacy of interim reclamation efforts and identify surface environmental concerns such as erosion and invasive species. As a result, BLM officials said some aspects of environmental protection might not be addressed during other types of inspections.

BLM officials said that the agency is considering making changes to its approach for prioritizing wells for environmental inspections. BLM's current criteria for prioritizing environmental inspections do not take into account when a well last received an environmental inspection, if ever. This approach differs from BLM's approach to production inspections, which considers the last inspection date in prioritizing production inspections.[45] The officials said that whether a well has received an environmental inspection in the last 5 years is being considered as a new prioritization factor for environmental inspections. BLM officials said they expect to complete updates to their approach for prioritizing environmental inspections by 2015.

---

[44]U.S. Department of the Interior, BLM, *2011 Inspection and Enforcement Internal Control Review of Documentation of Inspections and Review of Drilling, Environmental, and Production Inspections* (Washington, D.C., 2011).

[45]Production inspections are performed on wells that produce oil or gas to ensure that equipment, practices, and procedures adhere to the regulations, orders, and any applicable approval documents. Generally, specially trained petroleum engineering technicians, petroleum accountability technicians, or petroleum engineers conduct these inspections.

| Inconsistent Documentation of Inspections and Enforcement Actions | BLM's 2011 internal assessment also found that some environmental inspections of oil and gas wells and any resulting enforcement actions did not have adequate documentation in accordance with BLM's inspection and enforcement handbook.[46] Our site visits and interviews with BLM staff found similar problems. For example, we found that staff in some field offices do not document in AFMSS verbal warnings to operators to address environmental violations or problems. According to BLM's inspection and enforcement handbook, a verbal warning is a nonwritten communication to an operator for a violation or problem that will be corrected immediately prior to the inspector leaving the location and must be documented in AFMSS. However, some environmental staff said they prefer to handle environmental violations or problems informally, and that documenting all environmental violations or problems in AFMSS would be difficult given competing demands on their time. BLM officials acknowledged that such practices are not consistent with current agency policy. As a result of BLM's inconsistent documentation of violations or problems, it is difficult for BLM to (1) determine the extent to which they have occurred and whether the level of violations or problems has changed over time; (2) track whether corrective actions were taken; or (3) identify trends in an individual operator's history of environmental violations or problems and use this information to help prioritize environmental inspections. |
| BLM Faces Staffing Challenges | In some locations, BLM also faces challenges in retaining its oil and gas staff and in hiring new employees, including staff responsible for environmental inspections and enforcement. For example, management officials at the 11 field offices we contacted reported having some difficulty in hiring or retaining environmental protection staff. Difficulties reported included some environmental protection positions going unfilled for long periods and new staff hired often being inexperienced and requiring greater supervision, limiting their effectiveness. Field office management attributed the difficulties in hiring and retention to a variety of factors including a high cost of living in some areas, limited cultural opportunities, the remote locations of some field offices, and competition from industry. Also, according to BLM officials, some environmental staff |

---

[46]BLM's *2011 Inspection and Enforcement Internal Control Review of Documentation of Inspections and Review of Drilling, Environmental, and Production Inspections* also found similar problems with nonenvironmental inspections, such as production inspections, and nonenvironmental enforcement actions. Our review did not cover these types of inspections or enforcement actions.

prefer to be specialists in fields such as biology or botany rather than generalists, so they take other positions in BLM when they become available. BLM officials said that staff turnover and staff inexperience impact both the number of environmental inspections that can be conducted and the quality of environmental inspections and enforcement actions that are taken. For example, BLM officials said that it may take years for newly hired environmental staff members to complete training and be able to function without additional supervision, and once fully trained, they are frequently offered higher salaries in industry than BLM can pay.

In 2011, we added Interior's management of federal oil and gas resources to our high-risk list based, in part, on BLM's persistent problems in hiring, training, and retaining sufficient staff to meet its oversight and management of oil and gas operations on federal lands.[47] For example, in 2010, we found that BLM experienced high turnover rates in key oil and gas inspection and engineering positions, potentially affecting their oversight of oil and gas development on federal leases. In 2013, we updated our high-risk list and reported that the bureaus responsible for oversight and management of federal oil and gas resources on federal lands and in federal waters—including BLM—have encountered persistent problems in hiring, training, and retaining staff.[48] [49]

Conclusions

BLM has taken or initiated various actions in recent years to improve its processing of APDs, including implementing the Federal Permit Streamlining Pilot Project established under section 365 of the Energy Policy Act of 2005. BLM reported in 2008 that additional staff provided by the Pilot Project helped some offices improve their processing of APDs, but BLM has not finalized an updated assessment of the results of the Pilot Project since that time. The act required BLM to submit to Congress by 2008 a report that included a recommendation to the President on

---

[47]GAO, *High-Risk Series: An Update*, GAO-11-278 (Washington, D.C.: February 2011).

[48] GAO, *High-Risk Series: An Update*, GAO-13-283 (Washington, D.C.: February 2013).

[49]We are currently reviewing the extent to which BLM, the Bureau of Ocean Energy Management, and the Bureau of Safety and Environmental Enforcement continue to face problems hiring, training, and retaining staff to provide oversight and management of oil and gas, including whether the bureaus have identified the causes of their human capital challenges, the actions taken in response, and how they plan to measure the effectiveness of such actions.

whether the Pilot Project should be implemented throughout the United States, such as by expanding to all field offices, but BLM has not done so. In its 2014 budget justification report, Interior proposed several changes to the Pilot Project's statutory provisions and its funding mechanism; as of May 2013, Congress had not acted on this proposal, and the Pilot Project's future is uncertain. Without additional information from BLM on the Pilot Project, including a recommendation from the agency and updated information on the project's results, Congress may not have the information it needs as it considers the future of the project and its related funding.

The Energy Policy Act of 2005 also established a deadline for BLM to approve or defer completed APDs, but problems with the completeness and accuracy of BLM's data prevent an assessment of the agency's compliance with the deadline. Without such data, BLM also cannot accurately determine how much time it spends during the first period of the APD review process where BLM works with operators to provide necessary information to complete the APD, or during the second period where BLM reviews the completed APD. In April 2013, BLM issued new guidance regarding APD data entry, but it is unclear at this time what impact the guidance will have on the quality of BLM's APD data. In addition, AFMSS stops tracking some data for approved APDs when they expire or are rescinded, cancelled, or withdrawn. BLM would be in a better position to evaluate its performance and find ways of improving the efficiency of the permitting process or reducing the time it takes to process APDs if its APD data were more completely and accurately entered and retained in AFMSS, as well as in any new system that replaces AFMSS.

BLM increased the number of environmental inspections it performed on federal oil and gas wells and facilities from fiscal years 2007 to 2012, but the agency's environmental inspection prioritization process does not effectively ensure that the wells posing the greatest environmental risk are identified as high priority for environmental inspections. In part, this is due to challenges that BLM staff face obtaining information from AFMSS to prioritize wells for environmental inspections and because BLM staff do not have sufficient information on wells that have never received an environmental inspection. Further, BLM's process for prioritizing wells for environmental inspections does not consider when, or if, a well last received an environmental inspection. BLM would be in a better position to ensure that wells posing the greatest environmental risk are prioritized for environmental inspections if its staff were better able to obtain the information they need to do so from AFMSS, and from any new system that replaces AFMSS, and if information on the environmental inspection history of wells were included in the prioritization process. Furthermore, BLM is not consistently documenting environmental violations or problems found during the inspections that are conducted. Inconsistent documentation of environmental violations or problems and related enforcement actions makes it difficult to determine whether environmental compliance by operators is improving and limits the ability of BLM offices to find the information they need to prioritize future environmental inspections.

Recommendations for Executive Action

We recommend that the Secretary of the Interior direct the Director of the Bureau of Land Management to take the following four actions:

- Complete and submit to Congress a final report that outlines the results of the Federal Permit Streamlining Pilot Project to date, and makes a recommendation on whether the Pilot Project should be implemented throughout the United States, to meet the mandate of section 365 of the Energy Policy Act of 2005.

- Ensure that all key dates associated with the processing of APDs are completely and accurately entered and retained in AFMSS, and in any new system that replaces AFMSS, to help BLM assess compliance with required deadlines and identify ways to improve the efficiency of the APD review process.

- Take steps, including making changes to AFMSS, and in any new system that replaces AFMSS, to improve the ability of staff to identify wells that are a high priority for environmental inspection and to incorporate information on the inspection history of wells into the environmental inspection prioritization process.

- Take steps to ensure that environmental violations or problems and enforcement actions are documented in a consistent manner.

Agency Comments and Our Evaluation

We provided a draft of this report to the Department of the Interior for review and comment, and Interior provided written comments, which are summarized below and reprinted in appendix II. In its comments, Interior generally agreed with our report's recommendations. However, the agency stated that it noted some technical errors and incomplete information within the report relative to the oil and gas data that BLM maintains and its identification of high-priority environmental inspections. We incorporated BLM's technical comments as appropriate.

BLM had no comments concerning our first two recommendations. In regard to our third recommendation that BLM take steps, including making changes to AFMSS, and in any new system that replaces AFMSS, to improve the ability of staff to identify wells that are a high priority for environmental inspection and to incorporate information on the inspection history of wells into the environmental inspection prioritization process, Interior stated that it recognized that the inspection history of a well is an important factor to consider when assessing risk related to environmental compliance. Further, the department stated that in fiscal year 2011, it developed a new risk-based strategy for its oil and gas inspection and enforcement program in which risk factors are assigned to each type of inspection that BLM performs. For environmental inspections, one of the risk factors that field offices must consider is when an environmental inspection was last conducted on a well and that under the strategy, higher risk ratings are given to wells that have never had an environmental inspection or have not had an inspection for an extended period of time. However, the department said the environmental inspections component of the risk-based strategy has not yet been implemented because of limitations with the current AFMSS database and that the department is planning to transition to a new database system that will, among other things, have the ability to support the risk-based strategy for environmental inspections. According to Interior, the first phase of the new database system (related to APD processing and tracking) is expected to be implemented by the end of calendar year 2013, but the department did not specify when additional phases of the new system will be implemented to be able to support the risk-based strategy for environmental inspections. We appreciate the department's effort and mention in the report that it is considering making changes to its approach for prioritizing wells for environmental inspections. However, delays to the implementation of the new database system hinder staff's ability to identify wells that are a high priority for environmental inspection and to incorporate information on the inspection history of wells into the environmental inspection prioritization process.

In regard to our recommendation that BLM take steps to ensure that environmental violations or problems and enforcement actions are documented in a consistent manner, Interior stated that incomplete documentation of environmental inspections was included in the findings of an Internal Control Review of 10 field offices with major oil and gas responsibilities conducted by BLM in fiscal year 2011. The Internal Control Review report made recommendations regarding documentation of enforcement actions and inspections that Interior said the 10 field offices are in the process of implementing. In addition, the department stated the Internal Control Review report has been shared with all BLM State Directors. As our findings are consistent with those of the Internal Control Review, we reiterate the importance of BLM taking steps to ensure that environmental violations or problems and enforcement actions are documented in a consistent manner. We look forward to seeing how BLM addresses our recommendation.

As agreed with your offices, unless you publicly announce the contents of this report earlier, we plan no further distribution until 30 days from the report date. At that time, we will send copies to the Secretary of the Interior, the appropriate congressional committees, and other interested parties. In addition, this report will be available at no charge on the GAO website at http://www.gao.gov.

If you or your staff members have any questions about this report, please contact me at (202) 512-3841 or ruscof@gao.gov. Contact points for our Offices of Congressional Relations and Public Affairs may be found on the last page of this report. GAO staff who made key contributions to this report are listed in appendix III.

Frank Rusco
Director, Natural Resources and Environment.

Appendix I: Objectives, Scope, and Methodology

This appendix details the methods we used to assess the Department of the Interior's Bureau of Land Management's (BLM) management of the development of federal oil and gas resources. Specifically, the objectives of this report were to determine, from fiscal years 2007 to 2012, (1) what changes have occurred in BLM's oil and gas permitting workload; (2) what actions BLM has taken to manage its oil and gas permitting workload and what challenges, if any, remain; and (3) what actions BLM has taken to mitigate the surface environmental impact of developing federal oil and gas resources and what challenges, if any, remain.

To conduct our work, we reviewed relevant laws, regulations, and BLM guidance. We also interviewed officials in BLM headquarters and officials from a nonprobability sample of 11 BLM field offices and 4 BLM state offices.[1] We selected field offices based on their different geographical locations and the different types of oil and gas resources they manage, and to reflect varied levels of oil and gas permitting and environmental inspection activity and a mix of offices that are or are not participating in the Federal Permit Streamlining Pilot Project. Specifically, we visited and interviewed officials in 8 BLM field offices (Colorado River Valley, Little Snake, and White River in Colorado; Moab, Price, and Vernal in Utah; and Pinedale and Rock Springs in Wyoming) and interviewed officials by telephone in 3 additional field offices (Carlsbad and Farmington in New Mexico, and the North Dakota Field Office). In fiscal year 2012, these offices accounted for about 68 percent of all APDs received by BLM for federal oil and gas resources and for about 52 percent of all environmental inspections performed by BLM. During our site visits to the Colorado River Valley, Vernal, and Pinedale Field Offices, we observed BLM officials conduct environmental inspections of oil or gas wells and related facilities. In addition, we interviewed officials by telephone in 4 BLM state offices (Colorado, New Mexico, Utah, and Wyoming), which were selected based on their jurisdiction over 10 of the 11 field offices we contacted.[2] We also interviewed representatives from environmental organizations—the Western Organization of Resource Councils and the

---

[1] Because this was a nonprobability sample, observations from interviews with these offices, taken alone, do not support generalizations about other offices. However, such observations provide illustrative examples of the types of challenges BLM faces in managing its permitting workload and mitigating the environmental impact of oil and gas development.

[2] We did not interview officials from the BLM Montana State Office, which has jurisdiction over the North Dakota Field Office.

Upper Green River Alliance—and energy industry organizations—the American Petroleum Institute, the American Exploration and Production Council, and the Western Energy Alliance—to obtain their perspective on BLM's management of the oil and gas permitting process and on the implementation of BLM's environmental inspection and enforcement program.

In addition, we requested and analyzed electronic BLM data from Automated Fluid Minerals Support System (AFMSS) on federal oil and gas wells. We obtained data on applications for permit to drill (APD) received by BLM from fiscal years 2005 through 2012, environmental inspections performed from fiscal years 2005 through 2012, and data on all federal wells managed by BLM, including information on their last environmental inspection, if any, recorded in AFMSS. We assessed the reliability of these data by (1) performing electronic testing for obvious errors in accuracy and completeness; (2) reviewing existing documentation about the data and AFMSS; (3) interviewing BLM officials knowledgeable about the data; and (4) verifying with agency officials a limited sample of some of our results. On the basis of our assessment, we determined that the data we obtained were sufficiently reliable for our purposes to determine the number of federal wells managed by BLM. However, a BLM official knowledgeable about AFMSS said that BLM's environmental inspection data in AFMSS were not entirely reliable for fiscal years 2005 and 2006, primarily due to issues stemming from the Cobell Indian Trust lawsuit that resulted in the temporary shutdown of BLM's information technology (IT) systems.[3] As a result, BLM officials said they were unable to enter information into AFMSS on federal oil and gas wells, including information on APDs and environmental inspections, for several months in 2005. According to the officials, BLM field offices entered much of the backlogged information into AFMSS after the shutdown ended, but some data from fiscal years 2005 and 2006, particularly data on environmental inspections, were never entered into AFMSS due to the shutdown and the subsequent backlog of data entry the field offices faced in 2006.

---

[3]In the Cobell class-action lawsuit, which concerned the government's management of Native American trust funds, a U.S. District Court Judge on December 5, 2001, ordered Interior to disconnect from the internet all IT systems that house or provide access to individual Indian Trust data. Specifically, Interior's IT systems were impacted multiple times starting in 2001, and were shut down for several months in 2005 for federal data and until 2008 for Indian Trust data.

We preliminarily analyzed the environmental inspection data for fiscal
years 2005 and 2006 and shared the results with some of the field office
staff we interviewed, who confirmed that the data for their offices
appeared to be incomplete, but they did not know what the correct
numbers should have been. Consequently, we determined that the
environmental inspection data for fiscal years 2005 and 2006 were not
sufficiently reliable for our purposes, and we limited the scope of our data
analysis on environmental inspections to fiscal years 2007 through 2012.
We similarly limited the scope of our data analysis on APDs to fiscal
years 2007 through 2012 to be consistent with our presentation of the
environmental inspection data, and to focus this analysis on the years in
which BLM's revised permitting rule was used. In addition, since the
shutdown of BLM's IT systems for tracking data on oil and gas
development on Indian Trust lands lasted until 2008, we limited the scope
of our data analysis to federal oil and gas activities, and we did not
include Indian Trust oil and gas information in any of the well, APD, or
environmental inspection data presented in this report. In some offices,
such as the North Dakota Field Office, activities related to Indian Trust
wells can represent a sizeable portion of the office's overall oil and gas
workload.

To determine how BLM's permitting workload has changed, we analyzed
the electronic data obtained from AFMSS to count the number of APDs
for federal oil and gas resources with a received date listed from the start
of fiscal year 2007 to the end of fiscal year 2012. Based on the results of
our electronic testing of the APD data and interviews with agency officials
about the data, we determined that the data were sufficiently reliable for
this purpose. As part of our analysis, we reviewed summary data that
BLM had provided us on received APDs to see how they compared with
our results and to corroborate our results when possible. We identified
differences between the numbers we calculated and BLM's summary
data on received APDs for some offices, but since BLM could not provide
us with additional information on its summary numbers, we were unable
to determine why those differences exist. We present the results of our
analysis on the total number of APDs received by BLM by fiscal year from
2007 to 2012 in figure 3, and our results for the number of APDs received
by BLM's 33 lead oil and gas offices in fiscal years 2007 and 2012 are
presented in table 1. To identify potential factors that may have
contributed to changes in BLM's permitting workload, we interviewed BLM
headquarters officials and representatives of energy industry
organizations to obtain their views.

To identify actions BLM has taken to better manage its oil and gas
permitting workload, we reviewed BLM guidance and documentation and
interviewed officials in BLM headquarters to discuss policy, procedural,
and other changes that BLM has implemented. To examine the impact of
these actions and to determine if BLM continues to face any challenges in
managing its permitting workload, we interviewed officials in 11 BLM field
offices that manage oil and gas development, including staff at the
managerial and nonmanagerial levels. We also analyzed electronic data
from AFMSS on approved APDs to assess the average number of days it
took BLM to process APDs from the date of receipt to the date of
approval. To calculate the average number of days in fiscal year 2012, we
obtained and analyzed data on 4,228 APDs approved in fiscal year 2012,
representing more than 99 percent of the 4,256 APDs for federal oil and
gas resources that BLM reported were approved that year. The data we
obtained from BLM did not contain sufficient information on the 28 other
APDs approved in fiscal year 2012 to include them in our analysis, and it
is unclear how the average number of days it took BLM to process these
APDs compared with the average number of days we calculated for fiscal
year 2012. Based on our electronic testing of BLM's data on approved
APDs and interviews with agency officials about the data, we found that
the data were not sufficiently reliable to determine the number of days it
took BLM to process APDs prior to fiscal year 2012. To determine
whether BLM maintains the data necessary to assess its compliance with
the required deadline to approve or defer completed APDs, we analyzed
data on nearly 27,400 approved APDs that listed an approval date in
AFMSS from fiscal year 2007 to fiscal year 2012. Based on a review of
BLM documentation, we determined that our analysis included
approximately 89 percent of all APDs for federal oil and gas resources
that BLM reported were approved from fiscal year 2007 to fiscal year
2012. We found that BLM's data were not sufficiently reliable to assess
the agency's compliance with the required deadline due to problems with
the completeness and accuracy of the data. To identify potential factors
that may impact the amount of time it takes BLM to process APDs, we
interviewed BLM headquarters officials and representatives of energy
industry organizations to obtain their perspectives.

Our examination of actions BLM has taken to better mitigate the
environmental impact of oil and gas development on federal lands
focused on actions in BLM's oil and gas inspection and enforcement
program. We reviewed BLM guidance and documentation and
interviewed BLM headquarters officials to discuss key policy and
procedural changes that BLM has implemented. To examine how these
changes have impacted BLM's oil and gas environmental mitigation

efforts and to determine if any challenges remain, we interviewed officials in 11 BLM field offices, including staff at the management level, natural resource specialists, and other specialists responsible for conducting environmental inspections. In three of these offices, we observed BLM staff conduct environmental inspections of federal oil and gas wells to better understand the role of environmental inspections in BLM's mitigation efforts and to identify the challenges BLM staff face in performing these inspections.

We also analyzed electronic data obtained from AFMSS to quantify the change in the number of environmental inspections performed by BLM from fiscal year 2007 to fiscal year 2012. To measure this change, we analyzed AFMSS data on environmental inspections performed on federal oil and gas wells and facilities that listed an inspection completion date from fiscal year 2007 to fiscal year 2012. We present data on the change in environmental inspections from fiscal year 2007 to fiscal year 2012, broken down by BLM's 33 lead oil and gas offices, in table 2. Based on information provided by a BLM official knowledgeable about the AFMSS data, we excluded some environmental inspections listed in AFMSS from this analysis due to concerns about the accuracy of the AFMSS inspection records. In most cases, the environmental inspection records we excluded indicated that the inspections had been performed on well sites where no surface disturbance had occurred as of the date of inspection. According to the BLM official, some of these records may represent on-site inspections that occurred during the APD review process and were incorrectly recorded in AFMSS as environmental inspections. In total, we identified and excluded from our analysis more than 2,800 environmental inspections listed in AFMSS as having completion dates from fiscal years 2007 to 2012 due to the data not being sufficiently reliable for our purposes. This included excluding more than 160 environmental inspection records from the 2007 totals presented in table 2 and more than 580 environmental inspection records from the 2012 totals presented in the same table.

In addition, we obtained and analyzed electronic data from AFMSS on all wells involved in developing federal onshore oil and gas resources, including data on each well's most recent environmental inspection recorded in AFMSS, if any, and data on when each well was originally drilled. The data we analyzed from AFMSS included wells that were in a producible or service status (i.e., wells that were physically and mechanically capable of producing oil or gas or that were used to support oil and gas operations through activities such as water disposal) and were located either on lands with surfaces managed directly by BLM (data current as of December 18, 2012) or on lands with surfaces managed by other federal, state, or private entities, but with mineral rights controlled by the federal government (data current as of November 30, 2012).[4] We identified wells using the well's unique 10-digit American Petroleum Institute number. We analyzed these data to determine the number of federal wells managed by BLM offices, which is presented in figure 1. We also analyzed these data to assess how many federal wells had no record in AFMSS of ever receiving an environmental inspection. We limited the scope of our analysis of wells with no environmental inspection records in AFMSS to approximately 60,330 federal wells located on lands with surfaces managed directly by BLM. However, we excluded some other wells located on federal lands managed by BLM due to challenges we encountered analyzing their data, and we also excluded wells that were located on lands whose surface are managed by other federal, state, or private entities, but which have mineral rights that are controlled by the federal government. In total, about 32,270 wells in these categories were not included in this analysis.

We conducted this performance audit from May 2012 to August 2013 in accordance with generally accepted government auditing standards. Those standards require that we plan and perform the audit to obtain sufficient, appropriate evidence to provide a reasonable basis for our findings and conclusions based on our audit objectives. We believe that the evidence obtained provides a reasonable basis for our findings and conclusions based on our audit objectives.

---

[4]The results we present from our analysis of these data do not include federal wells that had been abandoned or nonfederal wells that were located on Indian Trust lands.

Appendix II: Comments from the Department of the Interior

United States Department of the Interior

OFFICE OF THE SECRETARY
Washington, D.C. 20240

JUL 2 9 2013

Mr. Frank Rusco
Director, Natural Resources and the Environment
Government Accountability Office
441 G Street, N.W.
Washington, D.C. 20548

Dear Mr. Rusco:

Thank you for the opportunity to review and comment on the Government Accountability Office (GAO) draft report titled, "Oil and Gas Development *BLM Needs Better Data to Track Permit Processing Times and Prioritize Inspections*" (GAO-13-572). The GAO's draft report recognizes the Bureau of Land Management's (BLM) key responsibilities for administering the development of oil and gas resources on Federal lands.

The Department generally concurs with the GAO's recommendations. However, we noted some technical errors and incomplete information within the report relative to the oil and gas data the BLM maintains and its identification of high-priority environmental inspections. Please refer to the enclosure for a description of those items and the BLM's recommended changes.

We would also like to bring to your attention important improvements that the BLM has developed related to recommendations three and four. Recommendation three states:

> **Take steps, including making changes to AFMSS, and in any new system that replaces AFMSS, to improve the ability of staff to identify wells that are a high priority for environmental inspection and to incorporate information on the inspection history of wells into the environmental prioritization process.**

The BLM recognizes that the inspection history of a well is an important factor to consider when assessing risk related to environmental compliance. In FY 2011, the BLM developed a new risk-based strategy for its oil and gas inspection and enforcement (I&E) program in which risk factors are assigned to each type of inspection that the BLM performs. For example, for environmental inspections, one of the risk factors that field offices must consider is when a well was last inspected. Higher risk ratings are given to those wells that have not had an environmental inspection or for which an extended period of time has elapsed since the last inspection.

Due to limitations associated with the current Automated Fluid Minerals Management System (AFMSS) database, the environmental inspections component of the risk-based strategy has not yet been implemented. However, the BLM plans to transition to a new database system that will, among other things, have the ability to support a risk-based environmental inspection strategy. The BLM Directorate and the Department have approved the project, which is being

2

implemented in phases due to funding limitations. The BLM expects to implement the first phase of the new database system, which is the APD processing and tracking system mentioned in the GAO report, agency-wide by the end of this calendar year.

Recommendation four states:

Take steps to ensure that environmental violations or problems and enforcement actions are documented in a consistent manner.

Environmental inspections and enforcement are an important part of the BLM's onshore oil and gas I&E program. In Fiscal Year 2011, the BLM conducted an Internal Control Review (ICR) of its I&E program in ten field offices with major oil and gas responsibilities. The BLM transmitted the result of the ICR to the State Directors via an information bulletin. One of the findings from the ICR was that the BLM's AFMSS database did not contain complete documentation of environmental inspections. Missing documentation included incidents of noncompliance and entries of written or verbal orders issued by BLM oil and gas I&E staff to operators. The ICR report included recommendations for the field offices to ensure that enforcement actions and inspections are properly and timely documented in the official well file and in AFMSS in accordance with national policy (H-3160-5). These field offices have submitted and are currently in the process of implementing their corrective action plans to comply with the report's recommendations and ensure that environmental violations and enforcement actions are appropriately documented. In addition to the ten field offices that participated in the ICR, the report was also shared with all BLM State Directors. The State Directors were asked to ensure that I&E operations in their field offices were not experiencing issues similar to those outlined in the ICR.

The BLM's corrective actions to date and its ongoing efforts to strengthen the oil and gas I&E program through implementation of a risk-based inspection strategy will help improve its environmental inspection prioritization process and standardize the documentation of inspections and enforcement actions across BLM offices.

Again, thank you for the opportunity to review and comment on GAO's report. We appreciate the GAO's insights and recommendations. If you have any questions or concerns regarding this response, please contact Steve Wells, Chief, Division of Fluids Mineral, at (202) 912-7143 or LaVanna Stevenson, BLM Audit Liaison Officer, at (202) 912-7077.

Sincerely,

Tommy P. Beaudreau
Acting Assistant Secretary
Land and Minerals Management

Enclosure

Appendix III: GAO Contact and Staff Acknowledgments

GAO Contact	Frank Rusco, (202) 512-3841 or ruscof@gao.gov
Staff Acknowledgments	In addition to the individual named above, key contributors to this report included Kimberly Brooks (Assistant Director); Cheryl Arvidson; Elizabeth Beardsley; David Bennett; Cindy Gilbert; Michael Kendix; Dan Royer; Christine San; Kiki Theodoropoulos; and Joshua Wiener.

GAO's Mission	The Government Accountability Office, the audit, evaluation, and investigative arm of Congress, exists to support Congress in meeting its constitutional responsibilities and to help improve the performance and accountability of the federal government for the American people. GAO examines the use of public funds; evaluates federal programs and policies; and provides analyses, recommendations, and other assistance to help Congress make informed oversight, policy, and funding decisions. GAO's commitment to good government is reflected in its core values of accountability, integrity, and reliability.
Obtaining Copies of GAO Reports and Testimony	The fastest and easiest way to obtain copies of GAO documents at no cost is through GAO's website (http://www.gao.gov). Each weekday afternoon, GAO posts on its website newly released reports, testimony, and correspondence. To have GAO e-mail you a list of newly posted products, go to http://www.gao.gov and select "E-mail Updates."
Order by Phone	The price of each GAO publication reflects GAO's actual cost of production and distribution and depends on the number of pages in the publication and whether the publication is printed in color or black and white. Pricing and ordering information is posted on GAO's website, http://www.gao.gov/ordering.htm.
	Place orders by calling (202) 512-6000, toll free (866) 801-7077, or TDD (202) 512-2537.
	Orders may be paid for using American Express, Discover Card, MasterCard, Visa, check, or money order. Call for additional information.
Connect with GAO	Connect with GAO on Facebook, Flickr, Twitter, and YouTube. Subscribe to our RSS Feeds or E-mail Updates. Listen to our Podcasts. Visit GAO on the web at www.gao.gov.
To Report Fraud, Waste, and Abuse in Federal Programs	Contact: Website: http://www.gao.gov/fraudnet/fraudnet.htm E-mail: fraudnet@gao.gov Automated answering system: (800) 424-5454 or (202) 512-7470
Congressional Relations	Katherine Siggerud, Managing Director, siggerudk@gao.gov, (202) 512-4400, U.S. Government Accountability Office, 441 G Street NW, Room 7125, Washington, DC 20548
Public Affairs	Chuck Young, Managing Director, youngc1@gao.gov, (202) 512-4800 U.S. Government Accountability Office, 441 G Street NW, Room 7149 Washington, DC 20548

Please Print on Recycled Paper.